Leadership
and
Effective Management

Management Applications Series

Alan C. Filley, University of Wisconsin, Madison
Series Editor

Leadership
and
Effective Management

Fred E. Fiedler
University of Washington

Martin M. Chemers
University of Utah

Scott, Foresman and Company
Glenview, Illinois

For Decky, Tory, Robert, Carol, Michael, and Holden

Library of Congress Catalog Card Number: 73-77673
ISBN: 0-673-07768-3

Regional offices of Scott, Foresman and Company are located in Dallas, Texas; Glenview, Illinois; Oakland, New Jersey; Palo Alto, California; Tucker, Georgia; and Brighton, England.

Foreword

The Management Applications Series is concerned with the application of contemporary research, theory, and techniques. There are many excellent books at advanced levels of knowledge, but there are few which address themselves to the application of such knowledge. The authors in this series are uniquely qualified for this purpose, since they are all scholars who have experience in implementing change in real organizations through the methods they write about.

Each book treats a single topic in depth. Where the choice is between presenting many approaches briefly or a single approach thoroughly, we have opted for the latter. Thus, after reading the book, the student or practitioner should know how to apply the methodology described.

Selection of topics for the series was guided by contemporary relevance to management practice, and by the availability of an author qualified as an expert, yet able to write at a basic level of understanding. No attempt is made to cover all management methods, nor is any sequence implied in the series, although the books do complement one another. For example, change methods might fit well with managing by objectives.

The books in this series may be used in several ways. They may be used to supplement textbooks in basic courses on management, organizational behavior, personnel, or industrial psychology/sociology. Students appreciate the fact that the material is immediately applicable. Practicing managers will want to use individual books to increase their skills, either through self study or in connection with management development programs, inside or outside the organization.

Alan C. Filley

Preface

Leadership has a certain aura of magic and glamour which has made it a fascinating topic of dinner conversation, of philosophical treatises, and of empirical studies. The question of how we can get people to cooperate on a common task for the purpose of achieving a shared goal has always been a major problem for mankind. Concern with this question has mounted as the complexity of tasks in our civilization has increased to the point where relatively few jobs can be accomplished by the individual working alone. The cobbler, the blacksmith, the cooper, and the wheelwright have practically disappeared, and in their place we have industrial concerns which are considered small if they employ fewer than a thousand workers.

This book deals primarily with the leadership of task groups in organizational settings. Typically, groups of this nature are departments, committees, crews, panels, or similar subunits of larger organizations which assign the tasks, appoint the leaders, and evaluate the groups' performance. While we will consider some studies of relatively independent operating groups, our focus is primarily on leadership in management contexts. Although this book is not intended to be a "how-to-do-it" manual, it is addressed to the student of organizational processes as well as to the practitioner for whom the implications for managerial practice are of prime importance.

The problem of leadership can be roughly divided into three major questions. These are, first, how one becomes a leader; second, how leaders behave; and, third, what makes the leader effective. Since the third question is undoubtedly the most important for present-day management of organizations, we shall devote the major portion of this book to this problem. The answer is far from simple, and it is most unlikely that a book will ever be written in which we can spell out, step-by-step, the recipe which guarantees success. The manager who wishes to become an outstanding leader, like the executive who intends to improve the effectiveness of his organization's performance, has to understand more than a few simple rules. He will have to come to terms with Kurt Lewin's famous dictum that there is nothing as practical as a good theory. Only if we understand the underlying theoretical principles are we likely to know how to modify and improve the way leaders and their groups operate.

In writing this book, we have drawn heavily and freely upon the research of our colleagues at the Universities of Illinois, Washington, and Utah who collaborated on the development of the Contingency Model, and we have also built extensively upon the work of eminent colleagues at other universities whose contributions have enriched our thinking. We would like to give particular thanks to Cecil Gibb, Terence R. Mitchell, Delbert Nebeker, Alan C. Filley, Robert J. House, and Joseph A. Litterer for their critical comments; and to Arlene Chemers, Nancy Ann Denton, Linda Hastings, and Hortense Woods for their assistance with editorial and stylistic problems as well as for the preparation of the manuscripts in their numerous incarnations. Needless to say, words of appreciation and sympathy are due to our wives who had to listen to innumerable minor variations on the theme of this manuscript.

Most of the research presented in this book was made possible through the support of the Office of Naval Research under contracts ARPA order No. 454 NR 177–472, NONR 1834(36) at the University of Illinois, NR 177–472, N00014–67–A–0103–0012 at the University of Washington, and NR 177–473, N00014–67–A–0103–0013. We also appreciate the support of the University of Utah Research Committee for the studies conducted in Salt Lake City.

Fred E. Fiedler
Martin M. Chemers

Contents

Introduction

1

Our firm knowledge of leadership is both sparse and of recent origin. This is not for lack of interest. Society's stake in its leaders and in their performance is obvious. The impact of effective leaders is dramatically demonstrated over and over again on a national scale in every country's history and on a local scale in every organization's past.

The generalship of Alexander the Great, of Napoleon, of Robert E. Lee, and of George Patton decisively affected the success of their military campaigns. The political leadership of Elizabeth I, of Lincoln, and of DeGaulle profoundly influenced the histories of their countries. The business leadership of men like Henry Ford or Andrew Carnegie exemplifies the same point in the private sector. The organization without effective leadership is in trouble. The importance of good leadership has, therefore, always been recognized. Plato's *Republic* and Confucius' *Analects* deal with the problem. The concern with leadership has a long history, but its systematic study is of recent vintage.

Although the first empirical investigation of leadership was published in 1904, the major impetus to the field came during World War I. At that time, intelligence tests were used in massive attacks on the problems of officer selection and placement. Between World Wars I and II, the major interest was in the identification of leadership traits and the way in which men rise to positions of leadership. This concern gradually gave way to current questions of how people become effective leaders.

1

The overwhelming part of leadership research has been conducted in the United States, and the field is still dominated by English-speaking investigators. One reason for this interest in leadership in the United States and other English-speaking countries has, of course, been the financial support provided by such organizations as the Office of Naval Research, the Ford Foundation, and other military and private agencies.

A more basic reason, however, may lie in the political and social heritage of the Western countries, particularly of those with a democratic tradition. Where nobody but an aristocrat can rise to a position of leadership, there is not much point in worrying about selection and recruitment. There have been, of course, leaders who have risen from the bourgeoisie or the laboring class in such societies, but these have always been exceptional cases.

The idea that leadership positions are to be awarded on the basis of merit rather than birth, political affiliation, or race, though still not completely accepted even in the United States, is considered perfectly preposterous in some parts of the non-Western world. Why, for example, should a man hand over the management of his business to an unrelated stranger when his own son-in-law needs a job? Is not the happiness of his family more important than a few dollars of extra profit? Should he not reward a political henchman and ally rather than someone who did not support him? Is not a friend's loyalty of greater value than cold efficiency?

Of course, America does not represent a completely unfettered meritocracy. Warner and Abegglen's (1955) book pointed out that no less than 48 percent of American business executives at that time came from families, or married into families, which had a substantial financial interest in their company. In others words, even in the United States the best road to a managerial position—at least in smaller companies—was to be born into a family which owned 51 per cent of the stock, or, failing that, to marry into one.

It was once taken for granted that the son would inherit his father's business, and that a protégé of the ruling prince would be selected for positions of responsibility which would now be classified as managerial. Up until the disastrous Crimean War in the late nineteenth century, commissions in the British army were purchased by those who could afford them, and an officer's training ground was more often the drawing room than the battlefield.

It was only with rapid industrialization and the growth of large bureaucratic organizations in business and government that the need for new leadership was really felt. The aristocracies of Europe were reluctant to become involved with the ungentlemanly calling of trade, and the larger and increasingly more complex business organizations required substantial numbers of managers to staff their departments, plants, and offices. By the end of the nineteenth century it had become obvious that the selection of managers and military leaders could no longer be left to chance or to the accident of birth.

WHAT DO WE MEAN BY LEADERSHIP?

Although the terms *leader* and *leadership* are freely used in the literature as well as in everyday language, there is a great deal of misunderstanding of what we really mean by them. Before we go any further, therefore, it is essential to spell out some of the key definitions we shall deal with in this book.

In layman's language, the leader is someone who is a little larger than life, one who draws people to him like a magnet by "charisma." He is the person others want to follow, the one who commands their trust and respect, as well as their loyalty. This is, indeed, the picture of the emergent leader, the "Great Man" who captures the imagination as well as the admiration of those with whom he deals. These are the heroes others want to emulate.

Most of the world's work, however, is done by leaders who are more mundane. These are the managers of insurance offices and service stations, the chairmen of PTA committees, the foremen of production lines, the department heads, and the top executives of business and government organizations. When we talk about leadership, we must encompass the multitude of these supervisors and managers as well as the charismatic and heroic personalities.

What, then, do we really mean by the terms *leader* and *leadership*? It is illuminating to look at some of the ways that leadership has been defined by those who have worked in this area:

"Leadership is the exercise of authority and the making of decisions" (Dubin, 1951).

"Leadership is the initiation of acts that result in a consistent pattern of group interaction directed toward the solution of mutual problems" (Hemphill, 1954).

"The leader is the man who comes closest to realizing the norms the group values highest; this conformity gives him his high rank, which attracts people and implies the right to assume control of the group" (Homans, 1950).

"The leader is the person who creates the most effective change in group performance" (Cattell, 1951).

"The leader is one who succeeds in getting others to follow him" (Cowley, 1928).

"Leadership is the process of influencing group activities toward goal setting and goal achievement" (Stogdill, 1948).

Two important threads run through all of these definitions. The first is that leadership is a relationship between people in which influence and power are unevenly distributed on a legitimate basis. The power may be given to the leader by the consent of the group members, by a contractual work agreement, or by law, but it is his to exercise.

The second important thread is that there can be no leaders in isolation. If you want to know whether you are a leader, see if there is someone following you. And since one cannot really coerce people to behave in appropriate ways, leadership implies that followers must explicitly or implicitly consent to their part in this influence relationship. In effect, followers voluntarily relinquish to the leader their right to make certain independent decisions. The leader-member interaction thus involves some kind of psychological or economic exchange. In the business world, this is generally a wage or a salary. But there is also likely to be some "psychic income," such as security, the chance to do something unusual, the pleasure of a gratifying relationship with one's coworkers, or the sense of achievement when the group reaches an assigned goal.

The psychic income is likely to play a big part in leadership situations of long duration or in situations of stress. The leader is not only someone whose directions are followed in exchange for a few dollars per hour; he is also a person who becomes emotionally important in the lives of his followers. His approval or disapproval affects their self-esteem and feeling of well-being.

The emotional relationship is by no means one-sided, though. The leader also becomes involved with his subordinates, and it makes a difference to him whether he is liked or disliked, whether he is perceived as fair or unfair, and above all whether he has the support of his group in performing assigned tasks.

Leadership is an amazingly ego-involving activity, even in contrived situations. This can be seen in management training workshops, where seasoned executives are frequently asked to work together in a variety of situations involving intrinsically meaningless activities, to let each one see how he and others perform on various leadership tasks. The tasks might consist of solving puzzles, of writing a hypothetical position paper or a recruiting letter, or of engaging in a make-believe business activity of some sort.

Yet even when everyone is clearly aware that these role-playing exercises are not going to affect his career, the leaders and their group members become intensely involved. How well has their group performed? Is the task really fair? Did another group get some unintended advantage? The definitions of leadership generally fail to do justice to the emotional component saturating the relationship between leader and group member.

Why should leadership be such an emotion-laden issue? The explanations which have been proposed span the range of theoretical positions. A psychoanalytic formulation, proposed by Freud, views the leader as a father figure, as someone to whom the group members have transferred the feelings they have toward their fathers. These feelings are apt to include love, respect, and fear.

Others have seen the leader as a person who can help his group members satisfy their emotional needs. Whatever the explanation, however, there is little doubt that the leadership situation is more than a transaction based on an exchange of economic commodities (i.e., money for time and labor). It is, perhaps, more akin to the father-son relationship, as Freud has suggested, than it is to the relationship of salesman and customer or lawyer and client.

MANAGERS AND LEADERS

Since everyone whose work involves the direction and supervision of other people is in a leadership position, all managers who supervise people are leaders. However, some, like the manager of a stock room or a ticket office, manage *things* and may not have supervision over employees. In this case, obviously, they are not leaders.

Likewise, military officers may or may not supervise others. An intelligence officer, an adjutant, or the personnel officer of a small military unit may be the only man in his section. He may also be a staff officer or an advisor in an embassy. These men are not in leadership positions.

It should be equally obvious that many leaders are not managers. A man may have power and influence without having a formal managerial position: he may be an informal work-group leader; a union steward; the captain of a football team; or the chairman of a civic or church committee. On the other hand, while most managers are indeed leaders, the leadership functions they perform are only a part of their managerial job. Managers have to prepare budgets and negotiate with customers, superiors, and colleagues; they have to write letters, sign requisitions, and perform many similar functions which do not directly or even indirectly involve the supervision or the direction of subordinates. We do believe, however, that leadership represents one of the most important dimensions of managerial accomplishment. In Chapter 3, we discuss in greater detail the distinctions between leaders and managers, and the ways in which these distinctions affect managerial selection and effectiveness.

Leadership status and leadership performance

The failure to take into account the difference between leadership *status* and leadership *effectiveness* has generated considerable confusion. Most of the early research relevant to leadership was concerned with how an individual achieves a position of leadership, that is, with his leadership status. The underlying premise was that there are, in fact, personality traits and attributes which affect the likelihood that a particular individual will become a leader. We will deal with this question in detail later.

Another distinction which is relevant to leadership status is the difference between *emergent* leadership status and *formal* leadership status. As the terms imply, an "emergent" leader emerges in a previously leaderless group without the aid of institutional appointment. By contrast, formal leadership status is conferred upon the individual by the organization of which his group is a part. Elected leaders are usually included in this category. Interestingly enough, though, while the overwhelming proportion of all civic, industrial, and military leaders are formally appointed, most of the early research on leadership—and most of the layman's interest—focuses on leadership attainment and on the emergent leader.

This is not, perhaps, very surprising. Most of us are more interested in becoming executives, managers, or leaders in various political and voluntary organizations than in worrying very much about how effectively we are likely to function. The popular literature has, therefore, been especially concerned with how a person should act in order to *become* a leader. The prescriptions range all the way from the Boy Scout precepts of being fair, honest, and loyal to detailed advice on how to manipulate people. Famous examples of the latter are Machiavelli's *The Prince* and Dale Carnegie's famous book of the 1930s on *How to Win Friends and Influence People,* not to mention the sarcastic book and musical, *How to Succeed in Business Without Really Trying.*

What do we mean by effective leadership?

The definition of leadership *effectiveness* is a problem of overriding importance. It is also a problem on which leadership theorists differ quite strongly. When we talk about a good leader we sometimes confuse effectiveness with being a good person, acting in a leaderlike manner, being liked and accepted as an officer, or having satisfied subordinates. It is certainly appropriate to define good leadership in some of these different ways. However, we shall here talk about leadership effectiveness in terms of *how well the leader's group performs its assigned functions.* An orchestra leader must be evaluated in terms of how well his orchestra plays. A football coach is judged primarily by how many games his teams win. Conductors do not get paid for making musicians happy; coaches get fired for losing too many games, not for failing to build character.

An organization often sets goals other than maximum productivity. An organization may even decide, for example, that satisfaction of group members is more important than productivity. But a company which stresses the value of employee satisfaction while basing the manager's bonus on the year's profit statement tells us in very convincing fashion the goals it sets the manager. Many organizations —especially large bureaucracies—often favor organizational stability over maximum productivity or effectiveness, and the reward structure —who gets promoted and who gets raises—shows it. Whatever the goals of the organization, when a clear statement of the criteria is made, we can undertake investigations of the effectiveness of the leader in achieving the goals.

While we will also deal with the effects of leadership on such other phenomena as employee satisfaction, motivation, and organizational stability, the major focus of this book will be on leadership effectiveness in terms of group productivity. The overwhelming concern of most organizations is, in fact, to develop or to find leaders who will increase the success of the groups with which they work. This success is usually evaluated in terms of productivity or effectiveness, be this in the form of a football game score or a corporate profit-and-loss statement. It may mean success on one task or performance over a span of ten or twenty years. If it is the latter, the leader and the organization must obviously be concerned with retaining and motivating their employees. We do *not* mean that the only appropriate measure of leader effectiveness is production rate. If our concern is with overall organization functioning, factors which affect organizational efficiency through absenteeism and turnover, such as worker satisfaction and morale, clearly must be considered. However, a primary focus on satisfaction as the major criterion of effective leadership would be equally misplaced.

It must, of course, be recognized that the performance of the group depends not only on the leader but on a host of related factors as well. To mention but a few, we might need to know how well motivated the group members are, how intelligent or skilled they are, how well they are trained to perform their jobs, how good the tools and equipment are, and to what extent the organization backs up the leader. But while all of these factors do influence performance, by and large the leader's personality, his motivation, and his style of behaving seem to determine performance to a greater extent than do all the others, at least when we compare groups which work under comparable conditions. Other things being equal, it then seems reasonable to measure the leader's performance by his group's success, and this approach is amply justified by the consistent finding that the leader's motivational pattern predicts quite well how his group performs. Just which motivational pattern works best depends strongly upon the situation.

WHERE DO LEADERS FUNCTION?

Our discussion should have made it obvious that the group is the natural habitat of the leader, just as the organization is the natural habitat of the group. There are very few groups which do not have a leader, and it is difficult to speak of the leader who does not have a group. To be sure, there are colloquial uses of the term. A man might be called a leader in the field of bookkeeping, or a woman might be designated a fashion leader, but these usages identify the individual who is at the forefront of a particular area. He may be an opinion former, a pioneer in his field. He may or may not know whether he has a following. He may be in the position of Gregor Mendel, the "leader" in genetics who never acquired followers until many years after his death. The term *leader,* as we shall use it here, requires some direct superior-subordinate interaction with others, and this usually implies a group of individuals in face-to-face contact.

By the term *group,* we generally mean a set of individuals who share a common goal or fate. An event in the group's interaction which affects one individual is likely to affect others as well. The definitions commonly used in the social sciences talk of groups as aggregates of people, or collections of individuals who belong together in some sense, usually physical, and in which the individuals comprising the group not only affect one another's actions but in which they also perceive each other as belonging together. It is, therefore, improper to speak of a group as a purely physical entity. Whether a collection of people waiting for a traffic light to change is a group depends on whether or not these individuals see each other as a group, on whether or not they are treated as a group, and on whether or not they behave toward one another as members of a group.

Groups are, as we said before, almost always subunits of a larger organization. Consider, for example, the many departments, work crews, teams, panels, and task forces which are found in government, military, business, industrial, and academic institutions. We find very few groups which have a truly independent life. School teams, committees, and crews usually represent an organization. To be sure, there are some occasional bridge groups, some family clubs, and small independent businesses and shops which fall into the rare category of being completely outside an organization, though even small enterprises, once they exceed five or six employees, are likely to break down into subunits. In general, whenever there are two levels of supervision, we have two or more interdependent groups working on a common purpose. We define such a set of interdependent groups as an *organization.* Almost without exception, organizations of this type have designated (appointed rather than emergent) leaders.

Most organizations, and, of course, the groups which constitute them, have some explicit or implicit goals. Some of these groups are informal associations of employees which develop because certain people like and respect one another, or because they feel the need to defend themselves against organizational demands which they consider unfair. Most groups are put together by the organization to accomplish one of the organizational goals or to perform certain of its functions. In general, an individual is more effective than a group on a per-man-hour basis when a task can be accomplished by an individual. After all, getting people together is a lot of trouble and frequently turns out to be a thankless and time-consuming business. If something can be done by one person, it should surely not be assigned to a group. If a group is formed, it is usually because a specific task or function cannot be performed by one individual alone.

There are groups which exist specifically for furthering the individual's goals, such as educational or therapeutic groups, encounter groups, and seminars. The purpose of these groups is the individual's growth rather than the benefit of the organization. The main concern of this book is with groups and organizations which have assigned tasks and explicit goals.

For purposes of discussion, we can think in terms of Schein's (1965) definition of an organization as "a rational coordination of the activities of a number of people for the achievement of some common, explicit purpose or goal, through division of labor and function and through a hierarchy of authority and responsibility." This definition aptly summarizes many of the points we have already made:

A) Groups have goals which are usually set by the organizations in which they are embedded.

B) The division of labor and function into leaders and followers facilitates the achievement of group goals.

C) The entire concept of leaders, groups, and organizations implies the exercise of authority, power, or influence.

One last point about groups is in order and should be made explicit. Groups of individuals and groups of groups (i.e., organizations) imply a situation of reciprocal benefit. Group membership is, in effect, a social contract. Group members surrender some of their autonomy and independence to the leader or authority in return for benefits which they could not acquire alone. A leader who does not recognize that his authority flows from the consent of subordinates is doomed to an unhappy if not short-lived leadership experience.

The next chapters deal with the problem of how individuals

achieve a position of leadership, how leaders behave, and what factors in their environment affect their relations with group members. The second part of the book discusses what makes leaders effective. Guided by a particular theoretical orientation, the authors believe that effective leadership is the result of a matching of attributes of the leader with the demands and constraints of the leadership situation. Any theory which overemphasizes either leader attributes or situational features at the expense of the other cannot adequately explain the full range of leadership phenomena.

Much of the literature in the area of managerial effectiveness has taken a one-sided view, stressing one aspect of the person, situation, or process at the expense of others. This book offers a theory of leadership and managerial effectiveness which seeks to integrate person, process, and situation.

REFERENCES

Cattell, R. B. "New concepts for measuring leadership in terms of group syntality." *Human Relations* 4 (1951): 161–84.

Cowley, W. H. "Three distinctions in the study of leaders." *Journal of Abnormal and Social Psychology* 23 (1928): 144–57.

Dubin, R. *Human Relations in Administration: The Sociology of Organization, with Readings and Cases.* Prentice-Hall, 1951.

Hemphill, J. K. "A proposed theory of leadership in small groups." *Second Preliminary Report.* Personnel Research Board, Ohio State University, 1954.

Homans, G. C. *The Human Group.* Harcourt Brace Jovanovich, 1950.

Schein, E. H. *Organizational Psychology.* Prentice-Hall, 1965.

Stogdill, R. "Personal factors associated with leadership: A survey of the literature." *Journal of Psychology* 25 (1948): 35–71.

Warner, W. C., and J. C. Abegglen. *Big Business Leaders in America.* Harper & Row, 1955.

Who Gets to be a Leader?

2

How do you get to be a leader? What special abilities, what personality traits and aptitudes must you have to go to the top of the heap? Are there some ways in which we can identify the potential leaders, ways in which we can differentiate them from the followers? Can we predict who will rise to the executive ranks, and who will succeed or fail when he gets there?

Questions of this type, which have been asked as long as psychologists have been working in the leadership area, have no simple answers. They depend on many factors. Most people intuitively expect leaders to have some personality traits or attributes which set them apart. A moment of reflection tells us, however, that almost everyone is a leader in some groups and a follower in others, and that there are very few people who are leaders all the time or even most of the time. There are relatively few who are never leaders. Personality factors alone, therefore, cannot determine who becomes a leader, especially since some of the factors which determine who becomes a leader are quite outside the individual's control.

Many positions of leadership require a certain educational background and experience, though being at the right place at the right time helps. You cannot become the chief of a medical staff without a medical degree; you cannot become a school principal without some educational training and experience; but the junior executive in a company in which a large number of senior executives unexpectedly resign has a better chance of promotion than one whose superiors are all in the prime of life and intent on holding on to their jobs.

Whether personality traits and attributes help one rise to positions of leadership is an important question, as is the related question of whether we can identify the potential manager, and we shall discuss both of them in this chapter. At this point we can only say that because there are many aspects of the managerial position which are not directly related to leadership, it is somewhat easier to tell who will become a manager than who will become a leader. Given the structure of contemporary management, there may even be some personality traits that predict who will become a manager, if not who will become a productive and successful one.

WHY DO PEOPLE WANT TO BECOME LEADERS?

There are very few people who are forced to assume leadership positions against their will. Those who are not motivated to become leaders are generally left out of the running. A substantial number of men and women are simply not interested in assuming the leadership responsibilities which might be coming their way. The number of professors who turn down the opportunity to become department chairmen or deans is fairly large. The number of men and women who decide against seeking political office is legion, and a substantial number of employees decline the chance to be promoted to foreman's jobs or to the executive ranks. It is important to realize, however, that those who refuse a leadership position at one time might well take another one the next time. People are simply not motivated to become leaders in every possible organization, and the first question which needs to be asked here is why some people seek certain positions of leadership and avoid others.

We hear a great deal about the shortage of qualified leaders. Rarely, however, is there a shortage of men ready to step into leadership positions. Obviously, leadership must have a great deal to offer if there is this constant supply of those who are willing to devote themselves to the good of a cause. The candidates for high public office, as well as the aspirants for executive positions in the private or the public sector of the country, are many. It is worth considering, therefore, what attracts people to the leadership job, especially if we hope to attract the types of people who are best able to perform various leadership functions.

There is little doubt that the leadership position provides important satisfactions. The most salient of these is the economic advantage which the leader enjoys. In some organizations the top job may pay twenty times as much as the lowest-paid job. In some underdeveloped countries the pay and benefits of a top company executive or a high government official may be over one hundred times that of a common laborer. Without going into the question of whether we think an executive is worth this much, it is clear that somebody must think so. However, leadership is sought even when there are no financial rewards. Leadership gives power over others, and with this power comes the satisfaction that one can not only control the fate of others—either benevolently or despotically—but also have greater control over one's own life and destiny.

The most comprehensive answer to the question of why people seek leadership comes from a study by Hemphill (1961) which shows that a variety of circumstances motivate an individual to attempt leadership. First, there must be a promise of a large personal reward for the leader if and when the task is accomplished, although the reward need not be material. Second, the leader must feel that he can, in fact, succeed in accomplishing the task if he tries. Third, the leader must feel that the group supports and accepts him. Finally, the individual must believe that he has the required abilities or skills to get the job done.

A study by Bavelas, Hastorf, Gross and Kite (1965) clearly supports Hemphill's findings. Members of leaderless discussion groups were told that a green light on the table in front of them would go on to signify that trained observers considered the individual's comments to be valuable. Through a programmed sequence of light flashes, these experimenters were able to manipulate the total conversational output of group members who were originally low on a leader preference rating. The greater the encouragement, the more the person talked. The more he talked, the more likely it was that he would later be nominated by others as a leader of his group.

One major reason that many people do not attempt to lead is the fear that the group might reject them. This was shown in one study by Gruenfeld, Rance, and Weissenberg (1969) which experimentally varied the amount of the attention and agreement the group members gave to the leaders. They found a drastic reduction in all kinds of leadership behavior as social support decreased.

Rejection by the group can be painful and threatening to self-esteem. The fear of failing is a very potent deterrent, and the individual who feels that he has less chance to accomplish the job, or that he is less competent than others, will hesitate to step forward as a leader. A past history of success or failure in leadership situations, whether in the laboratory or in real life, is then likely to have a strong effect on the individual's willingness to assume new leadership positions.

While we tend to think of leaders as special people, the significant difference between the leader and the nonleader is much less than is commonly imagined. The person who is an enthusiastic leader on one occasion may be an enthusiastic follower on another. Hollander and Webb (1955) found that individuals who were most frequently chosen as followers also tended to be preferred as leaders. And Mc-Clintock (1963) showed that the leaders and active followers were more similar in behavior to one another than they were to group members who were relatively inactive participants. This finding was also reported by Nelson (1964), who studied an Antarctic station. Accepted leaders and followers were similar in their common orientation to teamwork and their respect for various forms and sources of authority. The difference between leaders and active nonleaders is apparently not very great. The more important difference lies in whether the individual is a participant or a nonparticipant in the group.

How, then, do we induce people to become leaders? One method is, of course, to offer financial and other benefits which will make the job attractive. More importantly, however, those who aspire to leadership seek dominance, they seek control, and they seek acceptance. We must make it possible for them to obtain some of these satisfactions. This, after all, is the price followers pay for leadership. In accepting an individual as a leader, they voluntarily give up some of their freedom to make decisions in order to achieve a common goal. The individual who finds it difficult to give up control will not be a very happy group member, and the individual who finds it painful to make decisions for other people will not find leadership very satisfying.

We can, of course, make it more likely that the prospective leader will be accepted by his group and that he will perceive himself as capable of fulfilling the tasks which we set before him. The member of the group who is clearly the most qualified will hesitate less in accepting a leadership position than one who sees others around him who are, or consider themselves to be, more qualified. For example, placing a younger and less experienced man in a position of authority over a group of older and more experienced men is likely to lead to difficulties. The situation may well demand that the younger man prove himself as more capable, and that he convince the older members of his group that he is, in fact, the most competent member of the group. Needless to say, this is not always easy. A person's ideas of his own worth may or may not correspond to objective reality.

Whether one is accepted by others depends to some extent upon the history of the group. Being the successor to a giant is always difficult. No one would have found it easy to follow John F. Kennedy or Abraham Lincoln. On the other hand, following in the wake of a failure or of someone who was utterly obnoxious, so that "anything is likely to be an improvement," makes it easier to be accepted.

Higher management can also facilitate acceptance by ensuring that the new person will have the organization's backing. It can carefully route information through the new manager so that he will be in a position to know what is going on. Inside dope, gossip, and information about policies which will affect his group are important commodities. In addition, the organization can increase the power of the new leader by approving his requests, by accepting his recommendations for promotions and raises, and by building him up in front of his subordinates. Finally, the organization which helps the new leader be accepted by his group will enhance his willingness to tackle successively more difficult and responsible tasks. In short, we must build a situation in which the potential leader believes he can successfully fill the leadership position and in which the rewards for successful leadership are attractive to him.

MAINTAINING ONE'S LEADERSHIP POSITION

As we have said, most of us occupy dozens of leadership positions, but how do we remain in a leadership position? The flippant answer is, of course, by not getting fired. But how not to get fired presents some interesting problems. It is obvious that the leader must fulfill, at least to a minimal extent, the requirements of the organization. Groups which fail to perform their functions usually are disbanded in time, even though every once in a while we hear about an office in a government agency which keeps operating after the job it performs is defunct.

From a psychological point of view, the problem of keeping a leadership position is complicated because the leader's authority does not derive solely from the organization. The mere fact that a person has been appointed to a leadership position does not automatically enable him to exercise his leadership functions. He must somehow translate this legitimate authority into group productivity. Authority does not just flow from the top down. A person does not have authority simply because somebody "gives" it to him. He has authority because he is accepted by his subordinates.

By and large, the American worker, subordinate, or committee member is quite ready to grant the legitimately appointed leader the right to give orders and to direct and evaluate his work. In one study of 32 consumer cooperatives (Godfrey, Fiedler, and Hall, 1959), it was found, for example, that the assistant managers in no less than 24 of the companies said that they would prefer their present general manager as a leader in a different situation. This suggests a considerable acceptance of the general managers' leadership. Similarly, in a study of military tank crews, 18 of 25 crews endorsed the leadership of their tank commander in a confidential preference rating. At the other extreme, it is also true that a group can make life so miserable for its leader that he will be unable to function. Groups which have sabotaged their manager's position are certainly not unknown.

What, then, does it take to maintain a leadership position? A leader in the typical work organization must be able to satisfy both the requirements of the organization which appointed him to the job and, to some extent, the needs of his subordinates. The foreman has been called "the man in the middle" because he must reconcile the sometimes incompatible demands of his superiors and his subordinates. This problem is illustrated by a well-known study of the American soldier (Stouffer et al., 1949, p. 408). Table 2–1 compares the way in which privates, noncommissioned officers, and officers thought noncoms should behave. For example, only 13 percent of the privates agreed that "a noncom will lose some of the respect of his men if he pals around with them off-duty." Three times as many officers, however, felt that this would be the case. Likewise, 10 percent of the men agreed that a noncom will gain respect by having his men work hard, while 42 percent of the officers agreed with this statement.

Differences in the expectations of the leader by his subordinates and his superiors are quite typical and not really too surprising. The subordinate wants his superior to look out for his welfare and to leave him in peace; the middle manager wants his first-level supervisor to get

TABLE 2–1.   Comparison of Privates, Noncoms, and Officers on Attitudes towards Noncom Behavior. Source: Stouffer et al., 1949, p. 408. Reprinted by permission of Princeton University Press.

	Privates (384)*	Noncoms (195)	Officers (31)
	(Percent who agree with each statement)		
Social Relations			
"A noncom will lose some of the respect of his men if he pals around with them off-duty."	13	16	39
"A noncom should not let the men in his squad forget that he is a noncom even when off-duty."	39	54	81
Disciplinarian			
"A noncom has to be very strict with his men or else they will take advantage of him."	45	52	68
"A noncom should teach his men to obey all rules and regulations without questioning them."	63	81	90
Work Supervisor			
"A noncom should always keep his men busy during duty hours, even if he has to make them do unnecessary work."	16	22	39
"The harder a noncom works his men the more respect they will have for him."	10	18	42
"On a fatigue detail, a noncom should see that the men under him get the work done, but should not help them do it."	36	37	68

* Numbers in parentheses are the numbers of cases.

the maximum productivity from the group, consistent with the prevailing standards of how employees are treated by the organization. Whether the supervisor at the first level of management will favor the employees or comply with the wishes of his own boss will depend at least in part on the degree to which he wants to please his boss, the degree to which he must obtain voluntary compliance from his subordinates, and the degree to which his personal needs call for close interpersonal relations with members of his work group.

The situation is somewhat less complicated in groups and organizations in which the leader's authority comes primarily from members of his work group. This is the case in informal organizations and in groups which elect their leaders. In these cases (of "emergent" leadership), the primary criterion for maintaining the leadership position is the satisfaction of group members. This presents no particular problem in groups which can agree on goals, and in which there is no conflict about the methods by which these goals are to be achieved.

Needless to say, unanimity of opinion about goals and methods is the exception rather than the rule, and here too, the leader finds himself in the middle—this time between two or more factions within his own group or constituency. For this reason, the tenure of the emergent leader is frequently short-lived. Whether the leader is formally appointed, or formally elected for a specified term of office, he has to rely on the acceptance of his authority by his group members. His directions can never be so specific and his supervision can never be so close that he can dispense with the willing cooperation of his subordinates to do a good job. The employee who plays dumb and does exactly what he is told to do, and no more, is a stock comedy character who manages to make his boss look like a fool. It clearly takes more to be a leader than a title and the power to order others around.

What, then, determines the degree to which the leader can count on his group's support? Hollander (1958) has suggested an important conflict implicit in the leader's position. On the one hand, he must conform to the group's norms and standards in order to gain their acceptance. On the other hand, leadership, by definition, implies doing new things, departing from past norms and behaviors. Leadership often involves having the group do something which it would not otherwise be doing, and accepting new standards of behavior.

Hollander suggests that the leader earns *idiosyncrasy credits* by his conformity to the group and by satisfying the group members' needs. He is the model for adhering to and upholding the group's standards. The more "idiosyncrasy credits" the leader has to his account, the greater will be his freedom to depart from the group's expectations. A university faculty will forgive many unpopular statements by a president who is able to attract endowments, raise faculty salaries, and keep the students happy. Similarly, Einstein could attend formal weddings in old and somewhat smelly sweatshirts, but most of us could not—at least not more than once!

According to Hollander, each time a leader deviates from group standards or norms, he uses up some of the idiosyncrasy credits he has built up by past conformity and satisfaction of member needs. Further deviations from the norms which make up the central core of the group's ideology will be very costly to the leader's credits. We tolerate a scientist who behaves or dresses eccentrically, but not a scientist who lies about his findings.

The maintenance of the leadership position rests, then, on a system of social exchange. The leader must satisfy the needs of the organization, and he must protect the group members from the organization when necessary; he must also enable the members to gain satisfactions which are otherwise outside their reach. In return, the group satisfies the leader's need for power, for prominence, as well as giving him the willing compliance which enables him to get the organization's work accomplished (Jacobs, 1970).

A FUTILE PRIMER IN HOW TO SPOT THE GOOD LEADER

Most of us believe that we possess the uncanny ability to identify outstanding leaders. This confidence in the ability to spot the "comers" is encouraged by the belief of many executives that they would not be where they are if (A) they were not excellent leaders and (B) they could not pick them. It may well be true that some executives and personnel men do have the intuition necessary to select good leaders for certain jobs. It is equally true—and considerably more relevant—that most executives do not, and that they share this lack of ability with psychologists, personnel men, and the rest of us mortals.

It is worth asking, first of all, why many executives think they are endowed with such abilities. One answer is that it is very difficult to determine in most situations how well a leader performed, and only rarely do we compare one leader with another. Getting the typical vice-president to say why a particular manager performs well is often like trying to nail jelly to a wall: He tells you that every manager's job is different, that it's not just how much one does but how he does it, and that whatever measure you suggest does not really capture the essence of managerial performance.

That vice-president is, of course, absolutely correct. What a manager does is indeed highly varied, and managerial performance is very difficult to measure. It is therefore essential that we realize the difficulties not only in predicting who will achieve positions of leadership, and who will perform well as a leader, but also in evaluating the selections once they have been made.

Training and experience seem to have little to do with the ability to select leaders. Interviewers, be they executives, psychologists, or trained personnel managers, are not much better than chance at picking effective executives, and they are frequently worse. Each interviewer tends to approach the job with his own idea of what a good executive should be like, what the executive's job will be, and what is needed.

Webster (1964) discovered that the interviewer tends to form an initial impression within the first four or five minutes, and that he tends to search for additional information to support and substantiate his hunches. Webster, Wagner (1949), Mayfield (1964), and others have demonstrated that interviewers often disagree with one another quite radically, that the candidate rated best by interviewer *A* is likely to be rated poorest by interviewer *B*. This means that a person's career may depend on which interviewer he happens to hit that day.

Similar disappointing results in predicting future behavior on the job have been obtained even where the interviewers were highly trained psychologists and psychiatrists selecting psychology trainees for the Veteran's Administration (Kelly and Fiske, 1951). Only when interviewers refrained from making inferences—in effect, when they minimized the importance of interviewing in the first place—did their predictions lead to some success. The most notable example is Ghiselli's (1966) study of interviewing potential stockbrokers. In interviews with 507 candidates, the best predictor turned out to be simply how much a man knew about the job for which he applied. Ghiselli's predictions were thus mainly based on screening out men who did not know what to expect in the stock brokerage business and had little idea of why they wanted to enter it. The best predictor of clinical success in the Kelly and Fiske (1951) study was the Strong Vocational Interest Inventory, a test which matches the candidate's interest patterns to patterns of men who had remained (or survived) in the particular field or profession. In general, therefore, interviewing is a poor way of selecting executives and tends to contribute more "noise" than true information about the applicant's chances for succeeding.

It is important to reiterate that good performance criteria are essential for rational selection. Given all the difficulties and inaccuracies of interviewing and testing, if the personnel manager at least knows what sort of person he is looking for, he has a better chance of finding him. This is especially true in business. Because the nature of a manager's job is diversified, exact criteria are extremely difficult to specify. Even when we do have some general idea of what traits are needed for a particular job, we cannot be sure which exact level of the particular trait is most beneficial. Suppose that we are picking first-line supervisors in a production department. We may know that we would like someone who has enough education so that he can easily handle the administrative aspects of his job, but exactly how much education is enough, and how much is too much? A person who is overeducated for the job is likely to become ineffective. Many unemployed scientists and engineers are turned down for jobs because the company is afraid that they are overqualified and will therefore become bored and dissatisfied.

Another selection danger is that of placing too much emphasis on the one or two criteria we think are important. A personnel director may believe that a foreman's success depends largely on having a pleasing personality. He may then end up picking individuals who have gone through life on charm rather than merit or effort. Without good criteria and sound follow-up studies, he will never learn whether his predictions are right or wrong, and he will therefore go right on making inaccurate selections.

ARE THERE LEADERSHIP TRAITS?

We have taken a rather pessimistic look at selecting leaders by interviews. What is the possibility that we can select leaders by means of leadership traits? By a trait we generally mean a personality attribute or a way of interacting with others which is independent of the situation, that is, a characteristic of the person rather than of the situation. If leaders are born and not made, why should we not be able to develop some tests which tap the individual's ability to lead others? Many business executives, military men, and laymen firmly believe that there are inborn qualities or attributes acquired early in life which make a person a good leader. What is the evidence?

There is certainly no lack of research addressed to the question. In fact, the search for leadership traits was the most important single activity with which leadership theorists concerned themselves before World War II. The truly remarkable success of the intelligence testing spurred by the needs of World War I led to a natural extension of interest in the measurement of other psychological abilities and traits. Personality test development flourished in the years between World Wars I and II. The number and type of personality attributes which were investigated spanned a wide range including intelligence, dominance, aggressiveness, masculinity, perceptiveness, scholarship, fluency of speech, judgment, decision-making ability, insight, and physical characteristics such as weight, height, energy, health, physique, athletic ability, and grooming.

In general, the findings were disappointing. Stogdill (1948) reviewed the literature and, in effect, gave this line of study the *coup de grace,* even though the search for leadership traits still continues on a very limited scale. It must be said, however, that some relationships between leadership attributes and leadership status were found. While the relationships were very weak, it may be worthwhile to report what evidence there is.

Since many findings were contradictory, Stogdill assessed the strength of various findings on the basis of the number of studies which reported similar findings. Two major conclusions were reached based on the existence of positive results from at least 15 studies:

"(a) The average person who occupies a position of leadership exceeds the average member of his group in . . . (1) intelligence, (2) scholarship, (3) dependability in exercising responsibilities, (4) activity and social participation, and (5) socio-economic status.

"(b) The qualities, characteristics, and skills required in a leader are determined to a large extent by the demands of the situation in which he is to function as a leader" (p. 63).

Positive evidence from 10 or more of the studies showed:

"The average person who occupies a position of leadership exceeds the average member of his group to some degree in the following respects: (i) sociability, (ii) persistence, (iii) initiative, (iv) knowing how to get things done, (v) self confidence, (vi) alertness to, and insight into, situations, (vii) cooperativeness, (viii) popularity, (ix) adaptability, and (x) verbal facility" (p. 63).

It should be stressed, however, that the findings were so tenuous that there is no real hope of using them to identify or to predict leaders in any practical situation. In fact, Stogdill concluded:

"A person does not become a leader by virtue of the possession of some combination of traits, but by the pattern of personal characteristics, activities, and goals of the followers. Thus, leadership must be conceived in terms of the interaction of variables which are in constant flux and change. The factor of change is especially characteristic of the situation, which may be radically altered by the addition or loss of members, changes in interpersonal relationships, changes in goals, competition of extra-group influences, and the like. The personal characteristics of the leader and of the followers are, in comparison, highly stable. The persistence of individual patterns of human behavior in the face of constant situational change appears to be a primary obstacle encountered not only in the practice of leadership, but in the selection and placement of leaders. . . . It becomes clear that an adequate analysis of leadership involves not only a study of leaders, but also of situations" (p. 64).

A subsequent review of the leadership literature by R. D. Mann (1959) concluded that a number of relationships between an individual's personality and his leadership status in groups appeared to be well established. In particular, intelligence, adjustment, and extroversion are related to leadership status, though Mann found the relationships to be very low. Even the intelligence score, which has been the most consistent predictor, was only poorly related to leadership performance.

The relevance of early studies to current investigations of leadership quickly becomes apparent when we look at some popular assumptions about leaders, such as "he is a born leader," or "a man who can lead in one situation can lead in another." Similarly, we are constantly exposed to the customs of the business community and of government in which a man who has been outstanding in a managerial position of one organization is often transferred or hired by another organization. The examples abound. General Eisenhower was appointed as president of Columbia University even though he had never held a managerial position in an academic institution. He was subsequently elected President of the United States even though he had never before held political office. General MacArthur was elected chairman of Sperry Rand Corporation, and during World War II, Gordon Gray, the former president of a railroad, became the head of the U.S. Veterans Administration. Unfortunately, there are no data which would allow us to keep a tally of the managers who switched and failed. It should be pointed out, however, that to the extent that leadership calls upon the exercise of certain administrative skills, it is reasonable to expect that some transfer of these skills to new positions should be possible.

Let us consider the two sides of the trait issue. The individual committed to the belief that there is a leadership trait, or a pattern of leadership traits, can point to the findings which show that intelligence, sociability, initiative, and other traits or attributes are related to leadership status. He can also point to a number of individuals who performed outstandingly well in a wide variety of leadership tasks. He can further claim that studies which are inconclusive cannot be taken as proof that leadership traits do not exist. After all, the investigators simply may not have been bright enough, they may have been insufficiently persistent, the true leadership trait or trait patterns may not yet have been identified, and he knows—and you know—of people who keep getting into leadership positions.

The person who goes along with Stogdill, Mann, and others would have to admit that there *are* some personality attributes like intelligence which are related to becoming a leader. The relationships are not large, however, and they are more likely to be incidental to leadership than central. Someone who is intelligent, sociable, tall, and competent is also known by more people and is therefore more likely to be selected for a leadership position.

It is certainly true, and perfectly understandable, that the individual who is seen by one group of people as trustworthy, intelligent, or willing to assume responsibilities will probably look intelligent, trustworthy, responsible, etc., to another group of similar people. He will, therefore, be more likely to attain another leadership position, as has been demonstrated in a number of studies as well as in many everyday situations.

The question is whether the individual who *looks like* a leader and is therefore chosen to fill a leadership job will also turn out to be an *effective* leader. In other words, will he really do what he is supposed to do, and will he do it as well as or better than others who are called upon to perform a similar task?

A position of authority certainly does not imply competence or excellence in the person exercising that authority. While a doctor may have numerous patients, this is no assurance that he is actually able to cure people. He may, in fact, be a poor diagnostician and an inept practitioner who, by means of a good bedside manner, manages to look and act the part of the outstanding physician.

More importantly, it is often too late or quite irrelevant to ask how a person got to a position of leadership once he has achieved it. People become leaders for any number of reasons, and very often the choice of a particular individual is quite fortuitous. What does concern us is the question of how to choose the person who will be effective or how to improve his performance.

Another question, whether we can select the effective leader on the basis of his psychological traits, is more difficult to answer. As before, there is no evidence that there are any particular traits which make a person an effective leader. An individual's height and weight, or verbal fluency, may have assisted him in being elevated to a position of leadership, but the number of inches of height or the number of pounds of weight do not correlate with his performance.

The most telling piece of evidence against the leadership trait theory comes from a variety of studies in which the same leaders were observed or compared with others on different leadership tasks. The logic of this procedure is quite compelling. We may not know the nature of the particular leadership trait or of the personality attributes which make a man an effective leader, but *whatever they may be,* they should enable him to perform better over *many different situations.* As we said before, a leadership trait, like any other personality trait, is defined as an attribute of personality which is constant over situations. We should not call an individual intelligent if he can solve arithmetic problems in school but not in a business situation. We should not call him mechanically adept if he can work with gears but not with levers. Thus, if there is such a thing as a leadership effectiveness trait, the same people should emerge as effective no matter what the situation might be.

A number of important studies indicate that this is not the case. One study showed that the ratings of navy officers while on shore duty were totally unrelated to the ratings of these same officers on shipboard duty. Thus, effectiveness in one situation was quite unrelated to effectiveness in another situation.

Fiedler and his associates (1966) conducted a large field experiment in cooperation with the Belgian navy. It involved the assembly of 96 different three-man teams, each of which were given four identical tasks. One of these tasks consisted of writing a letter urging young men to join the Belgian navy as a career. The second and third tasks consisted of trying to route a ship convoy through 10 and then through 12 different ports in the most efficient manner (i.e., covering the least number of miles). The final task required the leaders to teach their men, without speaking, how to disassemble and reassemble an automatic pistol. All of these tasks were developed with the assistance of Belgian navy officers in charge of the camp, and the men participating in this study considered the tasks fair and appropriate.

The performance of each team was carefully measured and the performance scores for the four tasks were then intercorrelated to determine whether the leaders who performed well on one task would also perform well on the others. The results showed that the median correlation[1] was only 0.14, i.e., few ndividuals performed consistently well or poorly.

Similar results were obtained in other studies (Fiedler and Chemers, 1968). In fact, one major investigation of bomber crew performance during the Korean War, by Knoell and Forgays (1952), showed that there were no consistently effective commanders on such apparently similar tasks as visual bombing and radar bombing, and no relationships between bomber crews in the effectiveness of performing such tasks as navigating accurately, bombing, or maintaining the plane.

The implications of these studies are quite clear. They cannot be shrugged off as being inadequate, or based on too small a sample of

1. *The statistical relationship reported here is the correlation coefficient. The correlation coefficient represents the degree of relationship or dependency between two scores or measures. The value of the correlation coefficient ranges from 0.00 to 1.00 and may be positive or negative. The size of the coefficient indicates the strength of the relationship, i.e., coefficients approaching 1.00 indicate increasingly stronger relationships, while those approaching zero indicate that the measures are essentially unrelated. A positive correlation indicates that a high score on one measure predicts or is related to a high score on another measure. A negative correlation indicates that a high score on one measure is associated with a low score on the other. For example, we might expect a fairly strong positive correlation between height and weight. The taller an individual is, the more, on the average, we would expect him to weigh. A negative correlation would be found, for example, between the external temperature in a city and the volume of heating fuel consumed, i.e., the lower the temperature, the higher the amount of fuel used. Finally, an example of a zero correlation might be between intelligence and amount of hair on one's head. These two variables should be essentially unrelated. In the statistic reported above, a correlation of +0.14 was found between the performance of a leader on one task with his performance on another task. Since this coefficient is very close to 0.00, it indicates a leader's performances on two different tasks are essentially unrelated.*

groups, or consisting of meaningless tasks. The findings must be interpreted as indicating that leadership performance on one type of task is essentially unrelated to leadership performance on another type of task. Therefore, leadership traits, or any personality traits, are not likely to have a large influence on the performance of different leadership tasks. This would mean that we cannot really speak of effective or ineffective leaders. Rather, a leader may be effective on one task and ineffective on another.

SITUATIONAL FACTORS

It seems relevant at this point to consider some important situational factors which determine whether a person is chosen for a leadership position. Leaving aside for the moment such personal attributes as the individual's ability, his educational and technical background, or the accident of being available at the right moment, what environmental effects influence who becomes a leader?

As we have already pointed out, leadership tends to be bestowed upon people who are motivated and visible. Hermits and those who fade into the wallpaper rarely get selected for political office or managerial jobs. But some equally accidental features of the environment also play a part.

Physical and geographical factors

In one of the best known series of psychological studies, Bavelas and his associates (e.g., Leavitt, 1951) conducted a number of experiments on how various communication networks affect group behavior. In the typical study, a group of five or six people sit around a large table. Each position at the table is separated from the others by panels so that the group members are unable to see or speak to one another. The panels have slots in them through which the participants can pass messages. By keeping certain slots open and keeping others closed, one is able to determine who can communicate with whom. For example, in the "circle," each person can communicate only with the neighbors to his right and left. In the "wheel," all communications must pass through the individual who occupies the center position in the communication net.

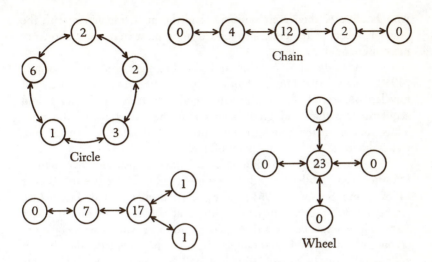

FIGURE 2–1. Communication Networks. Source: Leavitt, 1951. Copyright 1951 by the American Psychological Association and reproduced by permission.

      The groups in these communication net studies are usually given the task of solving a puzzle, or of reaching a joint decision. The finding which is most relevant for our discussion is that the individual in the center of the communication net, the nodal point of the system, is most frequently chosen as the most influential person.

      While this is in some respects a finding which is to be expected, since the group members must rely on the person who has most of the information, there is evidence from other studies that the conclusion also holds up under other conditions. Kipnis (1957) studied the effect of communication in B-29 bomber crews. These were heavy bombers designed for an eleven-man crew. Crew members spent a considerable amount of time in the plane, and many crews made a deliberate effort to socialize and to develop good crew relations even in their off-duty hours.

      The members of the crew were linked by the usual intercom system which allowed each person to speak to all others on the crew. Certain tasks, such as piloting and navigating the plane, making a bomb run, and deriving navigational measures, involved intense interactions among certain crew members, while others were required to stay off the intercom during these periods. Kipnis' study showed that the persons who, because of their crew positions, had the most interaction with the other members of the crew also tended to be most frequently chosen as most influential by them.

A study of a housing unit by Festinger and his associates (1950) showed that families living in the most central, and hence most traveled, section of the housing unit tended to have more friends and acquaintances than did families living at the periphery of the unit. Thus, here as in the bomber crew study, the individual with most contact is likely to be seen as most influential.

Even more surprising in some ways are studies by Steinzor (1950), Bass, Klubeck, and Wurster (1953), Howells and Becker (1962), and Sommer (1961). They showed that spatial, face-to-face arrangements of group members sitting at the same table can affect leadership emergence. In a three-person group in which two people are on one side of the table and one person is on the other side, the chances are that the singly seated individual will be seen as the leader. This advantage may well be due to the fact that it is easier to communicate with a person you face than with a person to whom you cannot speak without twisting your head to one side. The person sitting alone may also enjoy an advantage because, in our society, as well as in most others, the most important and most influential person generally sits at the head of the table. What is important here as well as in the other studies we have mentioned is the contribution which seemingly minor differences in the physical and geographical setting, or the frequency of communication, make in determining who becomes a leader. These physical factors play a relatively minor part, but they do affect leadership emergence.

Member characteristics

Besides such objective aspects of the situation as the communication structure, geographical focal point, or seating arrangements, a great deal depends upon the kinds of people who constitute the group. These are, after all, the ones who will select or reject an individual for the position of leadership. Several studies (Cattell, Saunders, and Stice, 1953; Cattell and Stice, 1954; Gibb, 1949, 1969) have shown that the personalities of members determine in part their choice of a leader. Autocratic leadership is more likely to emerge in groups which are high in intelligence and emotional maturity, but heterogeneous with respect to dominance needs. In other words, groups in which a few members are dominant and most of the members are submissive would find it easier to work under authoritarian conditions. These studies clearly indicate that the followers are not merely a background against which leadership emerges.

Considerable research (Sanford, 1951, 1952; Haythorn et al., 1956) has also shown that the authoritarian or democratic values of group members strongly affect the type of leader who is likely to emerge. Authoritarians prefer status-laden leadership with strong authority and direction on the part of the boss. Equalitarians are able to accept strong leadership if the situation demands it, but they do not prefer this type of leadership, and perhaps they need it less.

After reviewing the research, we can quite easily see why the search for a leadership trait was doomed before it had even begun. The endless array of conflicting findings results from the fact that the trait studies cut across situations with varying tasks, physical arrangements, and group compositions. It is undoubtedly true that the personality or motivational orientation of the leader plays its part, for it will affect the likelihood of his attaining a leadership position and the way he will behave in that position, and hence the likelihood of his success. On the other hand, ignoring the situational factors is somewhat like asking if it is a good idea to speak French. The answer depends on whether the speaker is in Paris, France, or Council Bluffs, Iowa, and to whom he is speaking.

CAN WE PREDICT MANAGERIAL PERFORMANCE BY PERSONALITY TRAITS?

On the basis of the evidence which we have presented so far it would certainly not seem very fruitful to predict leadership status or leadership effectiveness from personality traits. At the same time, a number of studies indicate fairly conclusively that we can predict to some extent the effectiveness of *managers* from personality tests and inventories. On the face of it, it seems inconsistent to say that leadership effectiveness cannot be predicted while managerial effectiveness can be, but as we have pointed out before, management involves a great deal more than supervision. Leadership and management are related but not identical.

An excellent discussion of the literature on selecting effective managers is presented by Campbell, Dunnette, Lawler, and Weick (1970), and the interested reader could do no better than to consult their analysis of the relevant studies. We will mention here only a few of the key findings in this area. These are of interest not only in showing that the prediction of managerial performance is possible to a limited degree, but also in pointing to the particular personal attributes which help to determine a man's success in the management area.

Harrell (1969, 1970) administered a battery of personality and interest inventories to students in the Graduate School of Business at Stanford University; he also obtained various intelligence and entrance test scores from their admissions records. Following up six to eight years later, he contacted the alumni and requested information on salary to judge each graduate's success. While salary may not be the best criterion of success in business, it is certainly one index if we assume that the more successful managers are likely to advance at a more rapid rate than the less successful ones, and that they will, therefore, also earn more. While Harrell's sample did not distinguish managers from nonmanagerial employees, he assumed that the majority of his subjects were in some type of managerial position.

Comparing the high and the low earners in big business, Harrell found 9 of 55 indices to differentiate at a statistically significant level. The high earners were more ascendant, they tended to have interests similar to those of personnel managers, they were more open-minded, more thoughtful, and they described themselves as more considerate. A companion study of high earners in small businesses (of less than a thousand employees) showed a similar pattern. They showed high energy and self-confidence, as well as being socially ascendant or bold. Personnel interests were again higher for the men who earned higher salaries. While there seem to be some personality differences, these findings might also indicate a greater awareness on the part of the high earner of what is expected in the job and a greater willingness to comply with society's expectations.

Another study by Ghiselli (1963) found that management performance ratings and the level reached by a manager in several organizations were significantly correlated with five ability and trait clusters. These were (A) intelligence; (B) supervisory ability, "the effective utilization of whatever supervisory practices are indicated by the particular requirements of the situation"; (C) initiative, which he sees as the motivation to act independently of others without their stimulation and support, as well as the capacity to see courses of action which are not readily apparent to others; (D) self-assurance, the degree to which the individual perceives himself to be effective in dealing with his problems; and (E) individuality, the degree to which he is dissimilar from the patterns characteristic of other individuals.

Korman (1968) questioned some of Ghiselli's findings, especially the relationship between intelligence and performance. From his own review, Korman concludes that intelligence is moderately correlated with performance for first-line supervisors, but becomes increasingly less related at higher managerial levels.

Nash (1965) showed that the more effective managers could be distinguished from the less effective managers on the basis of four interest components. These are (A) social service, humanitarian, and people-oriented interests; (B) persuasive, verbal, and literary interests; (C) a dislike for exclusively scientific, technical, or skilled trades; and (D) business contact and business detail activities.

Campbell et al. (1970) present a host of studies which support the notion that the effective managers do have different interest patterns, different abilities, and perhaps also some different personality traits. They conclude that as much as 30 to 50 percent of the predictable variance in managerial performance is due to individual differences, that is, that we can predict managerial performance from personality tests. We believe that this high estimate may be applicable only to a very limited number of organizations. Many studies show considerably poorer results and make us more cautious about the future of forecasting managerial performance by personality tests.

It must be remembered that the criteria of managerial success are usually not based on objective performance. Tenure, prior promotion, and salary level, all among the criteria most often chosen to indicate success, are highly influenced by a manager's compatibility with the system, especially his compatibility with his superiors. The psychological literature shows quite convincingly that compatibility and liking between individuals are based on the mutual perception of similarity in outlook, attitudes, goals, and values. In some organizations, a manager's chances for success may be strongly influenced by the extent to which he resembles in important ways other successful managers in the organization.

To the extent to which a profile of the successful manager can be developed, the method is based on the assumption that promising applicants will be similar to other successful managers. Promotion, salary advancement, and ratings of effectiveness are then at least in part dependent on factors which have little or nothing to do with a manager's actual performance. As Whyte pointed out in his book *The*

Organization Man (1956), and as has been shown by Vielhaber and Gottheil (1965), political beliefs, church affiliation, or club membership may well affect how readily a person is considered as eligible for promotion; although these attributes will not affect his performance in leadership positions. Thus, while it may well be possible to predict who will succeed in an organization, the prediction might still be poor if measured in terms of leadership effectiveness.

MANAGEMENT ASSESSMENT

In the belief that managerial performance can be predicted on the basis of personality trait patterns and attitudes, several large organizations have established elaborate programs for selecting successful managers by means of intensive personality assessment. These programs usually involve a period of two or three days during which the candidate for a managerial position is intensively interviewed and tested. Some programs also include various role-playing situations in which the candidate plays the part of an employee or a supervisor under given conditions. The assessment is then made by several personnel executives and psychologists, and sometimes psychiatrists, who pool their judgment about the individual's potential on the basis of the various test and interview data, as well as the background information which is available.

One large-scale program was conducted by the American Telephone and Telegraph Company. Berlew and Hall (1964), who directed the study, found that the success of managers can be predicted by assessment procedures and extensive psychometric tests. Thus, there is some promise that we can identify specific personality attributes and traits which managers require in specific organizations. The details of the Berlew and Hall findings are unfortunately not public (otherwise, of course, the aspiring executive could modify his answers in a way that would help him get promoted), and we thus have no way to judge the generality of the results obtained by these investigators. While there is clearly no reason to doubt the veracity of their report, it is impossible at this time to evaluate the theoretical and scientific implications of their work.

Campbell et al. (1970) summarized the results obtained by some major assessment programs, conducted at AT&T, IBM, and Standard Oil of Ohio, and by such organizations as the Peace Corps, which seem promising. They report, for example, that 31 of 62 men for whom success was predicted actually did reach middle management within 10 years. Of 63 college-trained men for whom the prediction was made that they would not reach middle management, only 7 did, in fact, reach that level. In a group of noncollege men, 15 of 41 who were predicted to reach middle management did so; only 5 of 103 men for whom the prediction was negative actually reached middle management.

Three facts must be borne in mind when interpreting the results of studies employing extensive test batteries for specific organizations. First, the procedure is quite expensive and time-consuming, requiring two or more days of the executive's time and a considerably greater number of man-hours by the assessment staff. Second, the success of the assessment procedure depends upon the professional competence of the assessment staff, and any substitution of nonprofessional assessors for qualified personnel is likely to lead to a considerable dilution of the results. Third, and probably most important, the programs and tests for the predictions of managerial performance are tailor-made for a particular organization with very specific requirements and possibly idiosyncratic criteria for judging performance and promoting management personnel. There is no assurance that the procedures developed by Standard Oil or Bell Telephone have any generalizability for, let us say, Ringling Circus, The JCPenny Company, the Illinois Central Railroad, or the Chase National Bank. To apply these, or any other, assessment procedures for selection or promotion of executives without intensive study of the specific company seems at this point indefensible as well as dysfunctional.

Peer ratings predicting leadership or managerial advancement have shown moderate success in industrial and military organizations (Campbell et al., 1970). The peer rating technique may here offer the advantage of obtaining judgments from many raters who interact extensively with the ratee and ostensibly know him better than an interviewer might.

SUMMARY AND CONCLUSIONS

We have tried to present in this chapter the factual evidence related to leadership identification and selection. To summarize, leader identification and selection is at best a haphazard undertaking and usually unproductive as well. There are many reasons for this:

1) Leaders' duties are highly varied and difficult to specify.

2) In many organizations superiors do not have very clear or accurate pictures of what subordinates are doing or what they should be doing.

3) Many factors might induce a person to attempt leadership, but there is no clear way to predict the attainment of that leadership position nor the effectiveness of the individual in that position. We know that we can raise the likelihood that an individual will seek a leadership position by making sure that the position offers appropriate rewards and opportunities.

In light of all we have said so far, it also seems likely that personality alone plays a relatively minor part in determining who attains leadership status, though a somewhat more important part in being selected as a manager. These data suggest that certain types of persons will succeed in a particular organization even though they may not be highly effective, and that a particular type of personality, a particular way of looking at life, or a particular set of interests may help a person advance in his particular organization. This may be because the individual fits the organizational requirements or perhaps only because his life style and his interests and attributes are congenial to his superiors who have control over who does and who does not get promoted. We will undoubtedly hear more on this issue in the course of the next few years.

REFERENCES

Bass, B. M., S. Klubeck, and C. R. Wurster. "Factors influencing the reliability and validity of leaderless group discussion assessment." *Journal of Applied Psychology* 37 (1953): 26–30.

Bavelas, A., A. H. Hastorf, A. E. Gross, and W. R. Kite. "Experiments on the alteration of group structure." *Journal of Experimental Social Psychology* 1 (1965): 55–70.

Berlew, D. E., and D. T. Hall. "Some determinants of early managerial success." Working Paper No. 81–64, Alfred P. Sloan School of Management, Massachusetts Institute of Technology, 1964.

Campbell, J. P., M. D. Dunnette, E. E. Lawler, III, and K. E. Weick. *Managerial Behavior, Performance, and Effectiveness.* McGraw-Hill, 1970.

Cattell, R. B., D. R. Saunders, and G. F. Stice. "The dimensions of syntality in small groups." *Human Relations* 6 (1953): 331–56.

Cattell, R. B., and G. F. Stice. "Four formulae for selecting leaders on the basis of personality." *Human Relations* 7 (1954): 493–507.

Festinger, L. "Informal social communication." *Psychological Review* 57 (1950): 271–92.

Fiedler, F. E. "The effect of leadership and cultural heterogeneity on group performance: A test of the Contingency Model." *Journal of Experimental Social Psychology* 2 (1966): 237–64.

Fiedler, F. E., and M. M. Chemers. *Group Performance under Experienced Leaders: A Validation Experiment.* Group Effectiveness Research Laboratory, University of Illinois, 1968.

Ghiselli, E. E. "Managerial talent." *American Psychologist* 8 (1963): 631–42.

Ghiselli, E. E. "The validity of the personnel interview." *Personnel Psychology* 19 (1966): 389–95.

Gibb, C. A. *The Emergence of Leadership in Small Temporary Groups of Men.* University of Michigan Microfilms, Publication No. 1392, 1949.

Gibb, C. A. "Leadership." In *The Handbook of Social Psychology,* Vol. 4, G. Lindzey and E. Aronson, eds., pp. 205–82. Addison-Wesley, 1969.

Godfrey, E. P., F. E. Fiedler, and D. M. Hall. *Boards, Managers, and Company Success.* Interstate Press, 1959.

Gruenfeld, L. W., D. E. Rance, and P. Weissenberg. "The behavior of task-oriented (low LPC) and socially oriented (high LPC) leaders under several conditions of social support." *Journal of Social Psychology* 79 (1969): 99–107.

Harrell, T. W. "The personality of high earning MBA's in big business." *Personnel Psychology* 22 (1969): 457–63.

Harrell, T. W. "The personality of high earning MBA's in small business." *Personnel Psychology* 23 (1970): 369–75.

Haythorn, W., A. Couch, D. Haefner, P. Langhan, and L. Carter. "The effects of varying combinations of authoritarian and equalitarian leaders and followers." *Journal of Abnormal and Social Psychology* 53 (1956): 210–19.

Hemphill, J. K. "Why people attempt to lead." In *Leadership and Interpersonal Behavior,* L. Petrullo and B. M. Bass, eds., pp. 201–5. Holt, Rinehart & Winston, 1961.

Hollander, E. P. "Conformity, status, and idiosyncrasy credit." *Psychological Review* 65 (1958): 117–27.

Hollander, E. P., and W. B. Webb. "Leadership, followership, and friendship." *Journal of Abnormal and Social Psychology* 50 (1955): 163–67.

Howells, L. T., and S. W. Becker. "Seating arrangement and leadership emergence." *Journal of Abnormal and Social Psychology* 64 (1962): 148–50.

Jacobs, T. O. *Leadership and Exchange in Formal Organizations.* Human Resources Research Organization, 1970.

Kelly, E. L., and D. W. Fiske. *The Prediction of Performance in Clinical Psychology.* University of Michigan Press, 1951.

Kipnis, D. M. "Interaction between members of bomber crews as a determinant of sociometric choice." *Human Relations* 10 (1957): 263–70.

Knoell, D., and D. G. Forgays. "Interrelationships of combat crew performance in the B-29." Research Note CCT 52–1, USAF Human Resources Research Center, 1952.

Korman, A. "The prediction of managerial performance: A review." *Personnel Psychology* 21 (1968): 259–322.

Leavitt, H. J. "Some effects of certain communication patterns on group performance." *Journal of Abnormal and Social Psychology* 46 (1951): 38–50.

McClintock, C. G. "Group support and the behavior of leaders and nonleaders." *Journal of Abnormal and Social Psychology* 67 (1963): 105–13.

Mann, R. D. "A review of the relationships between personality and performance in small groups." *Psychological Bulletin* 56 (1959): 241–70.

Mayfield, E. C. "The selection interview: A re-evaluation of published research." *Personnel Psychology* 17 (1964): 239–60.

Nash, A. "Vocational interests of effective managers: A review of the literature." *Personnel Psychology* 18 (1965): 21–38.

Nelson, P. D. "Similarities and differences among leaders and followers." *Journal of Social Psychology* 63 (1964): 161–67.

Sanford, F. H. "Leadership identification and acceptance." In *Groups, Leadership and Men,* H. Guetzkow, ed. Carnegie Press, 1951.

Sanford, F. H. "Research on military leadership." in *Psychology in the World Emergency,* J. C. Flanagan, ed., pp. 17–74. University of Pittsburgh Press, 1952.

Sommer, R. "Leadership and group geography." *Sociometry* 24 (1961): 99–110.

Steinzor, B. "The spatial factor in face to face discussion groups." *Journal of Abnormal and Social Psychology* 45 (1950): 552–55.

Stogdill, R. M. "Personal factors associated with leadership: A survey of the literature." *Journal of Psychology* 25 (1948): 35–71.

Stouffer, S. A., E. E. Suchman, L. C. Devinney, S. A. Starr, and R. M. Williams. *The American Soldier: Adjustment During Army Life*, Vol. I. Princeton University Press, 1949.

Vielhaber, D. P., and E. Gottheil. "First impressions and subsequent ratings of performance." *Psychological Reports* 17 (1965): 916.

Wagner, R. "The employment interview: A critical summary." *Personnel Psychology* 2 (1949): 17–46.

Webster, E. C., ed. *Decision Making in the Employment Interview.* Eagle, 1964.

Whyte, W. H., Jr. *The Organization Man.* Simon & Schuster, 1956.

How Do Leaders Behave?

3

As the hope of finding the magic personality trait faded, researchers turned toward the study of leader behavior. However, the legacy of the personality trait approach remained strong. If there is no single trait which can identify leaders or predict their effectiveness, is there perhaps a particular leadership style which makes groups and organizations effective?

By the term *style* we generally mean a relatively enduring set of behaviors which is characteristic of the individual regardless of the situation. Thus, leadership style, as this term is customarily used, is not really distinguishable from leadership traits. It differs primarily in focusing on what the leader *does* rather than what he *is*. The underlying assumption, that there is one ideal type of leadership behavior, is in fact still quite current.

The way in which managers lead is obviously important to the employee and to the organization as a whole. It makes a great deal of difference whether your manager tells you that you are doing an outstanding job and deserve a raise, or that you are incompetent and ought to be fired. How the manager behaves toward his subordinates affects labor turnover, employee satisfaction, and, of course, performance. In this chapter we will examine how the typical manager behaves and what types of behaviors might contribute to leadership performance and employee satisfaction.

We should, however, add the disclaimer that there is nothing about leadership which is simple, and the understanding of leader behavior is no exception. Managers do many different things. Some

of these specifically involve leadership functions, that is, the supervision of subordinates. Managers may also have nonsupervisory functions, and these may often be no less important as far as organizational
performance is concerned, but our primary concern in this chapter is
with *leadership* behaviors.

WHAT ARE LEADERSHIP BEHAVIORS?

First of all, there are no behaviors which are specific only to
leaders. Such typical "leadership behaviors" as directing, planning,
controlling, and supervising are also performed at one time or another
by individuals who are not themselves in leadership positions. An employee is frequently asked to prepare a work plan, to tell another how
to do his job, to inspect his work, or even to evaluate a fellow employee. By and large, most supervisors and their employees differ only
in the *frequency* in which they behave in certain ways.

The behavior of leaders will also vary considerably from situation to situation. The chairman of a board of directors, the production
manager, the foreman of a construction gang, and the director of a
research and development team will handle their subordinates differently. Despite these different leader behaviors, though, we are
almost always able to spot the supervisor of a group or the leader of a
crew when we walk into a work place. There are the inevitable trappings of office: "the name on the door and the rug on the floor," the
larger desk and more elegant furniture, and the extra telephone, as
well as a slightly different way of dressing which may set the leader
apart. In addition, people do not generally behave toward their supervisor as they behave toward fellow employees. They show more
deference, they wait until they are spoken to, they hesitate to break
into his conversation, they listen to him more intently. These differences in behavior of superior and subordinate are often subtle, and
they are therefore not always easy to measure.

The problem of studying leader behavior is made all the more
difficult because such critical leader behaviors as planning, directing,
and evaluating occur at rather infrequent intervals, and many of them
are difficult to define. The manager's order may be phrased in the
form of a question or suggestion, the evaluation may turn out to be
a smile or a pointed silence, and supervision often consists of quietly
walking through the office with an occasional stop to inquire how
things are going today.

What do leaders do?

One obvious method of finding out what occupies the leader's time consists of watching what he does. Observations of this type are, however, very costly in time and effort. Asking a busy person to keep a diary of his activities represents a considerable imposition on his schedule. Most people cannot or will not take time off during a hectic day to record everything they do, while writing down what was done at the end of the day leads to inevitable questions about selective recall of events. Some people remember things which were pleasant while others tend to recall those which were unpleasant. Some leaders have very good memories while others do not. Not many studies of executive behavior are available, but those which are certainly do bear out the commonsense observation that an executive does many different things and that he does them primarily with other people. Unfortunately, most of these are based on too few cases to give us much confidence in their conclusions.

A somewhat more adequate study, conducted by Horne and Lupton (1965), dealt with the activities of 66 managers from ten different firms. Detailed records were obtained of the time, place, and specific activity in which each manager engaged during one work week. The data came from the managers themselves, as well as from their secretaries and their assistants. Most of their time, 52 percent, was spent in their own offices, 11 percent in their own departments, and 6 percent in another department within their own companies. Forty-two percent of the activities involved transmission of information, only 9 percent involved any instructions, and 8 percent involved decision-making. Thus, these middle managers spent only 17 percent of their time in the typical leadership functions of directing and supervising.

One particularly interesting and important study on supervisory behavior (Nealey and Owen, 1970) was conducted in the psychiatric service of a large Veterans Administration hospital. The investigation focused on 25 head nurses, each of whom supervised a group of three to eight nursing assistants and one or two staff nurses and were in turn supervised by five unit supervisors. The unit supervisors reported to the chief nurse and the assistant chief nurse.

The study is unique in providing observations of managerial behavior from three different sources:

1) A Staff Activity Checklist provided a relatively objective measure of supervisory behavior. The experimenters made

20 instantaneous observations of each nurse in the sample. At randomly chosen points in time, the observer would come to the ward and write down what the nurse was doing. If he could not determine this clearly by watching her, he would check his rating with the nurse immediately afterwards. A checklist of fifteen nursing supervisor behaviors was broken down into three categories. These were (A) *supervision* of nursing assistants, (B) *direct patient care* (giving medicine, talking to patients, etc.), and (C) *administrative duties* (maintenance of supplies, preparing medicines, routine paper work, record keeping, meetings with hospital staff other than subordinates, etc.).

2) The head nurses responded to a questionnaire which asked them, first, to estimate the percentage of time they spent in each of the three categories listed on the Staff Activity Checklist and, second, how they thought they should ideally spend their time.

3) Each unit supervisor, that is, the head nurse's superior, was asked to estimate how much time her subordinates actually spent, and how much time they should ideally spend on work in each of the three categories.

One set of results provides an illustration: In over 75 percent of the observations, the head nurses were observed performing administrative duties. Yet, these same head nurses reported that they spent only 49.2 percent of their time in this fashion, while their superiors thought they spent 34.6 percent of their time on administration.

We find a similar discrepancy in supervisory behavior. The head nurses reported spending 25 percent of their time in supervising, while their superiors estimated that they spent 23 percent. But observed supervisory behavior occurred only 6.5 percent of the time. In fact, Nealey and Owen reported that 9 of the 25 head nurses were never seen supervising their subordinates during the 20 observation periods.

Finally, the unit supervisors thought that the head nurses spent 42 percent of their time in direct patient care, but the head nurses themselves reported that they spent 25.3 percent of their time caring for patients, while the observer reported only 17.4 percent of this behavior in his observations.

These major discrepancies raise some significant questions. If the superior does not know how much time his subordinate manager spends on an important aspect of his job, he will hardly be able to tell how much time his subordinate *ought* to devote to it. And if the superior has difficulty judging such objective aspects of his subordinate's job as time-use, how accurate is he likely to be in judging the overall quality of his performance?

Obviously, the superior will rate the manager's performance at least to some extent on what he thinks the manager ought to be doing with his time. The finding that the unit supervisor and the head nurse do not agree on how the head nurse actually spends her time is borne out by correlations of the reports of the head nurse and her unit supervisor. These were 0.28, 0.19, and 0.12 for supervision, direct patient care, and administration, respectively. These correlations show that the agreement was minimal. Let us now see on what basis the unit supervisor ruled the head nurse.

The actual behavior of the head nurse, as measured by the observer's Staff Activity Checklist, was completely unrelated to the unit supervisor's ratings. (A global performance rating by the unit supervisor correlated 0.01, 0.01, and −0.16 with time actually spent on supervision, direct patient care, and administration.) In other words, it did not really matter what the head nurse did, at least as far as the unit supervisor's ratings were concerned. It must be obvious that the supervisor cannot reward desirable behavior on the part of his subordinate managers unless he has a fairly good idea of what they are actually doing. It is equally obvious that such was not the case in the nursing organization in which Nealey and Owen collected their data.

How general is the condition which Nealey and Owen's study so vividly describes? From the few data available, it seems fair to predict that the situation is not uncommon. In a small unpublished study by Fiedler, government managers were asked to describe the time-use of their subordinate managers. The subordinate managers were similarly asked to indicate the way they spent their time on the job. The discrepancies were quite considerable and on the whole substantiate the Nealey and Owen findings. Another study by Cleven and Fiedler (1956) obtained actual productivity data on open-hearth shops in the steel industry. Ratings were obtained from shop superintendents and their assistant superintendents who evaluated the productivity of each melter foreman. The actual output data and the superintendents' ratings were unrelated. It is clear that we must use extreme caution in evaluating the various leader and manager behavior ratings, whatever the source of the ratings might be.

One further important point regarding time-use data needs to be stressed. The sheer amount of time spent on a particular activity may bear little relation to its importance, or even to the success of the task. For example, the amount of time students devote to study is essentially uncorrelated with their grades. Some students who are excellent scholars and get very high grades devote very little time to their studies, and some students, who spend all their time on their homework, end up with very low grades.

The unpublished study by Fiedler showed that middle managers spend almost one third of their time on routine administrative work—twice as much as time spent on any other category—yet the managers ranked this type of work only third in importance. The decision to develop a new type of car takes considerably less time than the design, the development of machine tools, the production, and the marketing, yet it is clearly an extremely important part of the process, as the histories of Ford Motor Company's successful Mustang on the one hand, and the ill-fated Edsel on the other, clearly demonstrate.

Critical incidents • We obviously need some measures which indicate the importance of a behavior rather than the time it requires. One technique for focusing on the more important aspects of managerial behavior is the Critical Incident Method developed by Flanagan (1954). These critical incidents are behaviors which qualified observers consider crucial to effective leadership performance. Flanagan collected over three thousand critical incidents of effective and ineffective behavior. These are short reports of episodes in which a leader performed especially well or especially poorly. Accounts are obtained from individuals who have held jobs similar to those being investigated, or from others who have worked in the situation as subordinates or superiors. On the basis of these incidents it is then possible to infer some of the qualities, abilities, or behaviors to be found in effective and ineffective leaders. Flanagan's study, for example, led him to classify important air force officer behaviors into the following six categories:

1) Handling administrative details.
2) Supervising personnel.
3) Planning and directing action.
4) Acceptance of organizational responsibility.
5) Acceptance of personal responsibility.
6) Proficiency in military occupational specialty.

A study by Williams (1956) illustrates the use of the technique in the study of management. This author collected over 3500 incidents of leadership behavior from 742 executives in various companies of different size and from different industry groups. These incidents were

TABLE 3–1.   Critical Incidents of Effective and Ineffective Managerial Behaviors. Source: Campbell et al., 1970, p. 80. Reprinted by permission of McGraw-Hill.

	Effective Incidents (%)	Ineffective Incidents (%)
1) *Planning, organization, and execution of policy* Communicates and interprets policy so that it is understood by the members of his organization Makes prompt and explicit decisions Perseveres in efforts to reach objectives	41	18
2) *Relations with associates* Assigns subordinates to jobs for which they are best suited Assists subordinates with personal difficulties as opportunities arise Supports policies and actions of superiors under all conditions (though he may privately disagree)	27	9
3) *Technical competence* Effectively organizes and applies knowledge of management to his job Utilizes all available sources of information in reaching conclusions or decisions Demonstrates ingenuity in solving management problems	4	7
4) *Coordination and integration of activities* Overcomes difficult obstacles to the achievement of objectives Makes vigorous attempts to reach objectives Fully supports and carries out company policies	8	31
5) *Work habits* Works diligently on delegated and self-assigned activities Works long hours when necessary to achieve assigned objectives Schedules his work and the work of his subordinates for efficient performance	19	23
6) *Adjustment to the job* Performs his work without apparent regard for personal advancement or compensation Fulfills commitments promptly Improves his proficiency by reading, discussion, research, and study	1	12

grouped into the six categories shown in Table 3–1, along with illustrative items.

The percentage figures indicate the proportion of incidents in each category associated with effective and ineffective managerial behavior. Planning, organization, and execution of policy followed by presumably good relations with associates, have the most frequent association with effective incidents. Incidents concerned with coordination and integration of activities and with presumably poor work habits were most often associated with ineffective managerial behavior.

What major inference can we draw from these incidents? The study tells us, for example, that the effective manager tends to make "prompt and explicit decisions," or that he "formulates effective policies to be used in achieving objectives of the organization for which he is responsible." It does not tell us how one should go about making such prompt and explicit decisions and how one formulates these effective policies. Nevertheless, the summary of incidents of effective and ineffective leader behaviors may suggest something about the types of problems which cause ineffective behavior, or situations in which effective or ineffective behaviors are likely to occur.

Behavior observations • The basic problem in observing leader behavior lies in the development of a system of categories which can be used for a wide range of groups and organizations, and which is related to important aspects of organizational behavior. One such system (Carter, 1953) showed that the leader made more attempts than other members to diagnose the situation and integrate and interpret what was taking place. Also, the leader more often gave ideas and initiated procedures for accomplishing the task. Finally, and perhaps most importantly, Carter and his associates found that behavior which characterized leaders in one task did not necessarily characterize them in another. His study was one of the first to question the concept of a universal leadership style which could be identified in terms of leader behaviors.

Couch and Carter (1952) discovered three major categories of behavior which accounted for most observed behaviors. These were (A) *Group Goal Facilitation,* that is, leader attempts to facilitate group task achievement; (B) *Individual Prominence,* meaning that the leader behaved in a way that would make him stand out in the group (i.e., he was influential, aggressive, and confident); and (C) *Group Sociability,* the degree to which the leader interacted socially with group members and tried to gain group acceptance.

Leader behavior descriptions

An extensive study at Ohio State University (Stogdill and Coons, 1957) resulted in the development of the Leader Behavior Description Questionnaire (LBDQ) which is now the most widely used method for describing leader behaviors. Based on statistical analyses of over 1500 behavior descriptions, two major factors, or interrelated sets of items, were identified. These have been labelled *consideration* and *initiation of structure*.

Consideration is described as the degree to which the supervisor shows concern, understanding, warmth, and sympathy for the feelings and opinions of his subordinates, and the degree to which he is considerate of their needs and welfare and willing to explain his actions. *Initiation of structure* subsumes behaviors which are related to the assignment of roles and tasks within the group, scheduling work assignments, defining goals, setting work procedures and standards, and evaluating the work of subordinates. Consideration and initiation of structure are uncorrelated in the typical group, although under some conditions high positive and negative correlations have been found.

These two behavior categories have some relationship to the "employee-centered" and "job-centered" behaviors which were identified by Likert (1961), as well as such other formulations as the Bales and Slater (1955) concepts of the socio-emotional and the task-specialist in small groups. Taking the research on leader behavior as a whole we can fairly say that these two supervisory and managerial behaviors, concern for the task and concern for the interpersonal relationship, appear to be solidly grounded in empirical evidence. The obvious next question is, therefore, how these two types of behavior relate to managerial performance.

The findings on the relation of initiation of structure to productivity are quite complicated. While there are some studies indicating that the effective leaders were both considerate and structuring (Fleishman, Harris, and Burtt, 1955), others give inconsistent results (Korman, 1966). Vroom (1960) cites eight studies with a positive relationship between considerate behavior and "productivity," two with a negative relationship, and one with no relationship. A study by Nealey and Blood (1968) showed that the effective head nurses of a psychiatric hospital were described by their subordinates as high in structuring behavior. However, the effective unit supervisors, the second-level managers, were described by the head nurses as low in structuring behavior.

The effective first-level supervisor in this setting gave clear instructions on how to do the job and set clear standards for her subordinates. The effective second-level manager, who supervised fellow professionals, did not.

Different types of situations obviously call for different types of behavior, and there is no reason to believe that a highly structuring leadership behavior will always be effective. Nevertheless, if we do not find a relationship between organizational performance and specific leader behaviors, we must be willing to ask whether there are relationships between leader performance and leadership styles, that is, to more general approaches to leadership.

LEADERSHIP "STYLES"

One of the first and most famous studies of leadership style was conducted by Lewin, Lippitt, and White (1939). These researchers formed a number of sponsored clubs among elementary school age boys. The leaders of these clubs were adult male graduate students in social psychology. Each leader was trained to behave toward the boys in his group in one of three leadership styles. The styles were *democratic,* in which group decisions were made by majority vote, equal participation was encouraged, and criticism and punishment were minimal; *autocratic,* in which all decisions were made by the leader, and the boys were required to follow prescribed procedures under strict discipline; and *laissez-faire,* in which the actual leadership activity of the group leader was kept at a minimum, allowing the boys to work and play essentially without supervision.

The groups with democratic leaders were the most satisfied and functioned in the most orderly and positive manner. The number and degree of aggressive acts were greatest in the autocratically led groups. The findings on group productivity are less clear. Lippitt and White (1943) report that the autocratically led groups spent more time in productive work activity than did other groups, but only when the leader was present. When the leader left the room, the amount of work-related activity dropped drastically. Further, all measures of productivity in the studies by Lewin and his associates refer to process variables, such as work-related conversation. No objective measures of productivity were ever assessed.

These findings cannot be interpreted as supporting the position that participative, permissive, human relations-oriented leadership styles will be universally effective. Two experimental studies by Morse and Reimer (1956) and Campion (1968) compared a hierarchical supervision program (directive, structuring) with an autonomy program (democratic, participative). The differences between these approaches were relatively small, although the hierarchical program resulted in greater profits due to lower labor costs.

Studies by Vroom (1959, 1960) indicate that employee characteristics determine at least in part which managerial style will be most effective. Employees high in authoritarianism and low in the need for independence were found to perform best under directive supervisors. Employees high in the need for independence but low in authoritarianism performed better under democratic leaders. Likewise, a study by Haythorn et al. (1956) showed that individuals who were themselves somewhat authoritarian were more satisfied with authoritarian leadership than were individuals who were not authoritarian. Perhaps these findings should not have been too surprising; all of us know people who function better and are happier when they know exactly what is expected of them, and when they have clear and precise instructions.

Another determinant of leader behavior is the expectations which others hold for us. Such social roles as leadership are in fact defined by the set of expectations which society holds for these positions. When a new manager joins an organization, he is often advised to "learn the ropes" before reorganizing his department. Learning the ropes simply means finding out how things are done or, in the jargon of the sociologist, "perceiving the relevant expectations surrounding the new role." Managers are dramatically reminded of the importance of role expectations when they attempt to function in a foreign culture. The position or job title in the new culture may be the same as at home, but the role expectations are often very different. For example, Chemers (1969) found that Americans see the good leader as either basically structuring or basically considerate; Iranians, on the other hand, want a benevolent, paternalistic manager who tells them exactly what to do.

Expectations can function similarly in our own culture. Company policy has a strong effect on supervisor attitudes. In companies which had authoritarian policies, Stanton (1960) found a more positive attitude toward "structuring" supervisory behavior than toward "consideration" behavior. In companies favoring more democratic policies, supervisors' attitudes were more favorable toward considerate behavior.

LEADERSHIP CLIMATES

McGregor (1960) has postulated two general types of organizational climates in terms of the role demands they place on the manager or supervisor. In the traditional, or "Theory X," organization, the manager's role prescription is built on the premise that workers are basically lazy, irresponsible, self-centered, and disloyal. This position, first credited to the Scientific Management theories of Frederick Taylor, calls for a directive, structuring, critical, and autocratic supervisor.

Almost diametrically opposed to Theory X organizations are the "Theory Y" organizations which McGregor favors. Theory Y is based on the premise that the worker's negative attitudes toward the organization are a result of the repressive nature of traditional organizations. A Theory Y manager's role prescriptions would stress democratic procedures, participative decision-making, and self-control. An important point of McGregor's theory is that he, like earlier theorists, postulates that the performance of the organization is a function of worker satisfaction and motivation. He argues, therefore, that Theory Y organizations and supervisors develop a work environment which maximizes human performance. The empirical evidence generally has failed to support this position.

Like McGregor, Rensis Likert and his associates have taken the view that traditional organizational influences on leadership have a deleterious effect on productivity as well as morale. Likert (1961) proposes a greater degree of participative management as a means for developing a supportive situation in which employees will be motivated to adopt the organizational goals. Quite clearly, organizations which publicly espouse and foster Theory Y principles are going to have an effect on leader behavior different from that of Theory X organizations. While there is some evidence supporting the principles of participative management, the benefits of this approach, as we shall see, are neither inevitable nor universal.

MANAGERIAL BEHAVIOR
AND SATISFACTION

Most of the research relating considerate leader behavior to subordinates' job satisfaction indicates a positive relationship. Likewise, the degree to which the manager allows participative decision-making is generally, though not universally, correlated with employee satisfaction. Fleishman and Harris (1962) found that, as the supervisors' consideration behavior increased, both turnover and grievance rates decreased, and that increases in initiation-of-structure behavior resulted in more grievances and higher turnover. Other studies have shown, however, that this relationship may not be general over other organizations. Thus, House, Filley, and Kerr (1971) showed that the much-quoted interaction between consideration and structure, as it affects employee satisfaction, does not appear to hold in research and development organizations in which the job is already very low in structure. In such organizations additional structure by the manager is more likely to help than hinder the work.

While the positive relationship of consideration to satisfaction has been generally confirmed, it must be questioned. For one thing, we are not sure of the direction of causality in these industrial field studies. It may well be true that a considerate leader makes his group members more satisfied, but the opposite might also hold. Satisfied and happy employees may elicit or perceive leader behavior which is described as considerate, and a person we like is more apt to be seen as considerate than someone we dislike. Vroom (1959) also makes another very important point: It is probably quite unreasonable to expect all employees in all situations to react similarly to particular managerial styles.

Two especially provocative studies should be mentioned. One, conducted by Turner and Lawrence (1965), investigated the relationship of employee satisfaction to job enlargement, or increase in the authority and responsibility which the employee was given and in the degree to which his job presented complicated, rather than routine and monotonous, problems. Somewhat surprisingly, a substantial number of employees preferred the routine, monotonous, and simple jobs; many of them did not want promotion or a more responsible position. Upon closer investigation, Turner and Lawrence found that the individuals who desired more responsible and varied jobs came from the less urbanized and predominantly Protestant regions surrounding the plants which they studied. The workers who wanted the routine jobs which did not require them to accept responsibility came from the predominantly Catholic, urban sections of the community.

While the temptation was considerable to relate these findings to the Protestant Ethic, Blood and Hulin (1967) have advanced a simpler explanation. Specifically, in a large study of archival records, Blood and Hulin classified work locations in terms of the community's alienation from middle-class norms. In relatively alienated communities, employees were less willing to accept responsibility and were more satisfied with routine jobs; employees in integrated communities felt more satisfied with positions in which they were given more discretion and with jobs which could be considered enlarged.

These and similar findings indicate quite clearly that the individual's background and, probably, his personality are critical factors in determining his job satisfaction. Some people apparently thrive in situations which provide them with challenging and responsible jobs, while others shrink away from them.

SUMMARY AND CONCLUSIONS

In this chapter we have tried to summarize some of the relevant research on the effect of leadership behavior on managerial performance and employee satisfaction. A number of studies have shown that the considerate leader who is employee-centered has effective groups. While the temptation is great to say that such leader behavior therefore increases the effectiveness of groups or organizations, a number of fairly obvious methodological questions must be considered. First and foremost, in the majority of the studies which show this relationship between considerate or employee-centered behavior and group performance, it is not possible to determine whether the leader behavior causes the group to be effective or whether the effective group causes the leader to be employee-centered. Both measures are usually taken at the same time. There is certainly no reason to believe that an effective group does not give considerable satisfaction to the leader and that the satisfied leader will not, therefore, be more considerate and concerned about the feelings and welfare of his subordinates. Moreover, the leader whose group has been highly effective is much more likely to ask for member participation in decision-making than one whose group has been ineffective or hostile to him as leader.

Most importantly, as we will show later on, there is considerable evidence that the behavior of leaders changes from situation to situation. The leader who may be quite employee-centered and considerate in situations in which he feels in complete control tends to become concerned with the task in situations in which his control of the group is minimal.

The second problem—the relationship between leader behavior and employee satisfaction—is equally difficult to disentangle. It seems perfectly reasonable to assume that the considerate leader and the leader who engages his subordinates in the decision-making process will have a more satisfied and congenial group. On the other hand, groups which are harmonious, which are satisfied, and which like the leader are more apt to describe him as considerate than are groups which are torn by conflict and which actively dislike the leader. Which is the chicken and which is the egg?

REFERENCES

Bales, R. F., and P. E. Slater. "Role differentiation in small decision-making groups." In *Family, Socialization and the Interaction Process,* T. Parsons and R. F. Bales, eds., pp. 259–306. The Free Press, 1955.

Blood, M., and C. Hulin. "Alienation, environmental characteristics, and worker responses." *Journal of Applied Psychology* 51 (1967): 284–90.

Campbell, J. P., M. D. Dunnette, E. E. Lawler, III, and K. E. Weick. *Managerial Behavior, Performance, and Effectiveness.* McGraw-Hill, 1970.

Campion, J. E., Jr. "Effects of managerial style on subordinates' attitudes and performance in a simulated organizational setting." Unpublished doctoral dissertation, University of Minnesota, 1968.

Carter, L. F. "Leader and small group behavior." In *Group Relations at the Crossroads,* M. Sherif and M. O. Wilson, eds. Harper & Row, 1953.

Chemers, M. M. "Cultural training as a means for improving situational favorableness." *Human Relations* 22 (1969): 531–46.

Cleven, W. A., and F. E. Fiedler. "Interpersonal perceptions of open-hearth foremen and steel production." *Journal of Applied Psychology* 40 (1956): 312–14.

Couch, A. S., and L. Carter. "A factorial study of the rated behavior of group members." Paper presented at the meeting of the Eastern Psychological Association, Atlantic City, N.J., April 1952.

Flanagan, J. C. "The critical incident technique." *Psychological Bulletin* 51 (1954): 327–58.

Fleishman, E. A., and E. F. Harris. "Patterns of leadership related to employee grievances and turnover." *Personnel Psychology* 15 (1962): 43–56.

Fleishman, E. A., E. F. Harris, and H. E. Burtt. *Leadership and Supervision in Industry.* Educational Research Monograph No. 33. Personnel Research Board, Ohio State University, 1955.

Haythorn, W., A. Couch, D. Haefner, P. Langhan, and L. Carter. "The effects of varying combinations of authoritarian and equalitarian leaders and followers." *Journal of Abnormal and Social Psychology* 53 (1956): 210–19.

Horne, J. H., and T. Lupton. "The work activities of 'middle' managers." *Journal of Management Studies* 1 (1965): 14–33.

House, R. J., A. C. Filley, and S. Kerr. "Relation of leader consideration and initiating structure to R and D subordinates' satisfaction." *Administrative Science Quarterly* 16 (1971): 19–30.

Korman, A. K. "Consideration, initiating structure, and organizational criteria: A review." *Personnel Psychology* 19 (1966): 349–63.

Lewin, K., R. Lippitt, and R. K. White. "Patterns of aggressive behavior in experimentally created social climates." *Journal of Social Psychology* 10 (1939): 271–99.

Likert, R. *New Patterns of Management.* McGraw-Hill, 1961.

Lippitt, R., and R. K. White. "The 'social climate' of children's groups." In *Child Behavior and Development*, R. G. Barker, J. S. Kounin, and H. F. Wright, eds., pp. 485–508. McGraw-Hill, 1943.

McGregor, D. *The Human Side of Enterprise.* McGraw-Hill, 1960.

Morse, N. C., and E. Reimer. "The experimental change of a major organizational variable." *Journal of Abnormal and Social Psychology* 52 (1956): 120–29.

Nealey, S. M., and M. R. Blood. "Leadership performance of nursing supervisors at two organizational levels." *Journal of Applied Psychology* 52 (1968): 414–21.

Nealey, S. M., and T. M. Owen. "A multi-trait-multimethod analysis of predictors and criteria of nursing performance." *Organizational Behavior and Human Performance* 5 (1970): 348–65.

Stanton, E. S. "Company policies and supervisors' attitudes toward supervision." *Journal of Applied Psychology* 44 (1960): 22–26.

Stogdill, R. M., and A. E. Coons. "Leader behavior: Its description and measurement." Research Monograph No. 88. Ohio State University, 1957.

Turner, A., and P. R. Lawrence. *Industrial Jobs and the Worker.* Harvard University Press, 1965.

Vroom, V. H. "Some personality determinants of the effects of participation." *Journal of Abnormal and Social Psychology* 59 (1959): 322–27.

Vroom, V. H. *Some Personality Determinants of the Effects of Participation.* Prentice-Hall, 1960.

Williams, R. E. "A description of some executive abilities by means of the Critical Incident Technique." Unpublished doctoral dissertation, Columbia University, 1956.

The Leadership Situation

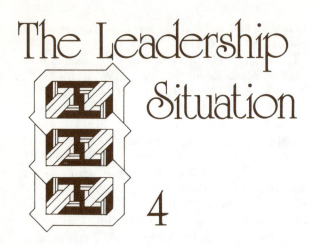

4

I am the master of my fate;
I am the captain of my soul.
Henley, *Invictus*

Ernest Henley's famous lines are very dear to our hearts. We like to think that we behave as we wish to behave. We are not, after all, puppets or robots. When a person does something, we tend to attribute it to his personality: "Joe gave to the Children's Fund because he is a kindhearted person," not because the situation would have been awkward if he had failed to give.

Personality, however, is not the sole determinant of behavior. It is all too easy to predict someone's behavior if we know only the situation in which it will be observed. The uniformity of behavior at a funeral, a ball game, or a cocktail party is striking. Most differences in the way people act are relatively minor when we consider how much of their behavior is determined by social context.

It is not too surprising, therefore, that the situation plays an important part in any attempt to understand leadership. The term *situation* generally refers to aspects of the environment which affect the individual. These aspects may be physical objects such as office furniture or they may be social relationships with customers, fellow workers, the boss, or subordinates. Finally, the situation may refer to such commonly held attitudes or perceptions in an organization as the custom of taking work home from the office, taking a twenty-minute coffee break, or the understanding that nobody ever gets fired. These are intra-organizational variables. Extra-organizational aspects of the situation may include a surplus or a shortage of labor, the number of competitors, or the location—suburban or urban—of an office.

ORGANIZATIONAL CLIMATE

Most of the emphasis in describing organizational climate has been on interpersonal aspects of the situation. Some writers have identified its components as the degrees of managerial support, concern for new employees, and conflict within or between departments of the organization (Schneider and Bartlett, 1968). Others have defined organizational climate as including organizational constraints and red tape, the degree to which the employee has independence to make decisions, the nature and frequency of rewards, challenge and risk, and warmth of support.

Campbell et al. (1970), in their review of the literature, identify four common factors in all investigations:

1) *Individual autonomy,* the individual's ability to exercise his responsibility, independence, and individual initiative;

2) *The degree of structure imposed upon the position,* the degree to which the objectives of the job, and the methods for accomplishing it, are established and communicated to the manager by his superiors;

3) *Reward orientation,* the degree to which the organization rewards individuals for hard work or achievement;

4) *Consideration, warmth, and support,* the support and stimulation received from one's superior.

Another important contribution to understanding the leadership situation was made by Burns and Stalker (1961), who defined organizational climate in terms of a mechanistic-organic continuum. Mechanistic organizations tend to have tightly knit hierarchical structures, rigid and formalized rules, low mutual trust among members, and a primarily downward communication flow. Organic organizations display loose structures, a multidimensional communication flow which is directed toward peers and superiors as well as subordinates, and a high degree of trust and tolerance in relations among co-workers. This classification permits us to view the organization in terms of structuring the individual's environment, although it overlaps, of course, with the dimensions of individual autonomy, degree of structure, and reward orientation identified by Campbell et al.

An important question is how organizational climate affects organizational performance. The evidence seems to show that a good climate reduces labor turnover and increases employee satisfaction but does not greatly increase organizational or group effectiveness (Brayfield and Crockett, 1955; Csoka, 1972). This conclusion flies in the face of the still common assumption that morale and worker satisfaction are essential to productivity, at least over the long run. Two points must be remembered in interpreting these findings. The first is that most investigations which relate group climate to group performance do not address the question of causality—does a good group climate result in good performance, or does good performance result in good group climate? Second, as Brayfield and Crockett (1955) and others have pointed out, there is no reason to assume that a supervisor will obtain greater work output just because he is liked. After all, he may be liked by his subordinates precisely because he does not make too many demands on them. Driving his men may please his boss but not his subordinates. Having autonomy and freedom to make decisions will be good for productivity only if the supervisor makes the right decisions.

Group task

One of the most important aspects of the situation is, of course, the purpose of the group or the organization—what is it supposed to do; what is its primary task? This has until fairly recently been a neglected problem in organizational and leadership theory, but there can be little doubt that it plays a major role in determining the leader's and the group member's behavior. McGrath and Altman (1966) pointed out that the most effective method for changing leader behavior simply consists of giving different instructions. You tell person A to do one thing and person B to do another, and lo and behold, they behave in a different manner. We previously assumed that a leader would behave and perform in a similar manner no matter what the task might be. Current research shows that this belief is not justified. Morris (1965), who investigated the behavior of 108 groups in a wide variety of tasks, estimated that about 60 percent of a leader's or a group's behavior can be ascribed to task differences.

One of the most important investigations in this general area was conducted by Woodward (1965) and her associates on 100 companies in England. She divided the companies in her sample, on the basis of their technology, into: firms with predominant unit and small-batch production; firms with large-batch and mass production; and firms with long-run process production of the same product. In unit production, articles were made either one by one or to the customer's individual order. Large-batch or mass production is best exemplified by assembly line production or a production system which requires a major retooling for each change in product. Long-run processes are illustrated by electric power generation, chemical processing, or petroleum cracking plants.

Woodward found that the successful organizations in the small-batch and unit-processing, as well as those in the continuous-flow category, gave managers more autonomy and freedom in designing their own rules than did the unsuccessful organizations. There were fewer written definitions of duties, greater delegation of authority, less closely organized groups, and less emphasis on organizational consciousness.

The middle-technology group used more managers in the production process and closer supervision of production personnel and emphasized written procedures, elaborate controls, and rigorously applied sanctions to assure discipline of the work force. Also, the span of control differed markedly in companies with different technologies. The median number of employees reporting to first-line supervisors in small-batch firms was 23, while in the large-batch companies one supervisor generally had no more than six or eight immediate subordinates.

The type of task now appears to have considerable bearing on the leader's contribution to performance. A foreman will have relatively little influence on the effectiveness of a moving-belt assembly line operation, while that of a research and development group, or of a team of script writers, may be influenced quite considerably by the leader's personality, ability, and supervisory behavior.

Exactly what do we mean when we speak of a task? According to Hackman (1969, p. 113), a task consists of a stimulus complex and a set of instructions which specify what is to be done with the stimuli. "The instructions indicate what operations are to be performed by the subject with respect to the stimuli and/or what goal is to be achieved." Hackman points out that the instruction to think would not constitute a task, whereas instructions to think about a specific picture and to interpret its meaning would be.

One carefully developed analysis of tasks by Shaw (1963, 1971) identified four major underlying factors. These are *task difficulty*, the amount of effort required to complete the task and the ease with which it can be done; *solution multiplicity*, the degree to which there is more than one correct solution to the task, the outcome can be defined, the task can be accomplished in different ways, and the task is intrinsically interesting; *cooperation requirements*, the need for group members to interact in order to perform the task; and *the population familiarity*, the degree to which the task would be encountered by the population at large.

The important feature of Shaw's typology is its emphasis on the degree to which the task is structured or unstructured, clearly defined or vague, with one best procedure or an infinite number of possible methods, in other words, on the extent to which the task itself determines what the leader is to accomplish and how he is to proceed. Of course, tasks which are equal in degree of structure may vary in level of difficulty (examples might be building a digital computer according to a blueprint versus assembling tricycles, or developing a new labor relations policy versus planning an office picnic). Again, the important question, as far as leadership theory is concerned, is how the task affects the leader's relationship with his subordinates.

Power, control, and influence

If we tried to characterize the leader-member relationship in a few key words, they would surely be power, control, and influence. Control and influence are important aspects of almost all interpersonal relations, whether we speak of parents trying to control their children, political candidates trying to influence the voter, or wives trying to influence their husbands. Bertrand Russell (1938) considered power the fundamental concept of the social sciences, in the same sense that energy is the fundamental concept of physics.

The most obvious way in which a leader obtains power is through the organization which gives him the right to direct, evaluate, reward, and punish within certain usually rather well defined limits. Within these boundaries the leader can expect the organization to support him. If an employee does not follow legitimate orders, the organization will administer disciplinary action or uphold the supervisor's right to discipline. Moreover, even though the foreman or first-line manager no longer has the power of his counterpart of fifty or sixty years ago, he still has a great deal to say about the fate of his subordinates. He is consulted on promotions and pay raises, and his praise and criticism carry a great deal of meaning in most situations.

The supervisor will be seen as more powerful the more his recommendations carry weight with higher management. Tannenbaum (1968) and his associates at the University of Michigan have shown that the attitudes and directions of the supervisor affect subordinates roughly in proportion to the backing the supervisor is able to get from his own bosses, even though his authority is limited. It generally does not extend over the employee's leisure time, his family, or friendship choices. It will vary from task to task. The chairman of a committee can only expect compliance with rules, not with orders to stay out of certain nightclubs. A ship's captain, on the other hand, has a considerably broader area of responsibility which may well extend to the off-duty time of his crew.

Being appointed by an organization is, of course, only one way in which individuals derive social power. French and Raven (1959), in their well-known analysis, call this "legitimate power." Other methods of control and influence include the power of rewarding and punishing and the expert's power of having information or control over information flow (Raven, 1965). Finally, there is "referent power," which is based on the personal relationship between leader and follower, specifically, the desire of the less powerful to identify with, and please, the more powerful person.

French and Raven, as well as others (e.g., Blau and Scott, 1962; Peabody, 1962; Harsanyi, 1962), have stressed that any power and influence relationship, including leadership, must be seen as an exchange in which both parties must give and take (Tannenbaum, 1968; Jacobs, 1970). The leader can be coercive, or punitive, provided he is also either personally attractive to his members or able to satisfy important needs his members might have. His power always depends at least to some degree on his acceptance by his group members and the group members' willingness to comply with his wishes. As stated by Filley and House (1969, p. 58) ". . . we need a somewhat different concept of authority. Under this concept, authority is not viewed in terms of rights of command; rather, it is explained in terms of one individual's willingness to accept direction from another." Barnard (1938, p. 163) further pointed out that "the decision as to whether an order has authority or not lies with the persons to whom it is addressed, and does not reside in 'persons of authority' or those who issue those orders."

The power an organization vests in a particular leadership position may, in fact, be quite illusory. This is particularly apparent when a manager supervises the work of highly trained experts and specialists. The adage that knowledge is power still holds true, but a problem in leadership emerges when the expertise is on the side of the subordinate rather than the supervisor. With our growing dependence on specialists and experts, this problem is a trend of the future where it is not already a reality today.

When a leader does not have the expertise to master the job, he can neither tell the subordinate how to do it nor supervise him to make sure that it is done right. He must then rely on his relationship with his subordinate (his referent power) or else he must be willing to provide something in exchange. This may not only be a higher salary, but it may also mean that the indispensable subordinate is allowed to "get away with things" for which others may be reprimanded and penalized—which may in turn invite problems with others who are not as indispensable.

It is also well to consider that two first-level supervisors in the same organization may have the same job but quite different power relationships with their employees. Consider here the position of a manager in an outlying branch office which is visited once or twice per month by the regional manager, in contrast to the manager who happens to have his office right in the headquarters building, and thus has the general manager dropping in on him every few days. The branch manager of the outlying office is practically autonomous compared to his colleague at headquarters.

Somewhat similarly, the foreman of a highly centralized "tall" organization may have five or six managerial levels above him, while a first-line supervisor in a "flat" organization may report directly to a vice-president. The supervisor in the flat organization will, therefore, find it relatively easy to influence top management, while the man in the tall organization may never see anyone above his boss's boss, so that his influence will be slight both in his own eyes and in those of his men.

The common assumption has been that the leader's power enables him to control the group more effectively and that the group will therefore perform better. This clearly has not been the case. A number of studies have shown that the more powerful leaders do not necessarily have more effective groups (e.g., Fiedler, 1966; Chemers and Skrzypek, 1972), and we must clearly look further than this attractive and plausible hypothesis.

SITUATIONAL FACTORS
AND LEADERSHIP THEORY

We have presented several attributes of the situation and we have undoubtedly left out many others, such as employee attributes, motivation, and abilities, which are just as likely to affect the behavior of the leader and of his group members. There is little doubt that the situation plays an important role in leadership performance, but we need to ask what specific features of the situation affect the leader.

We have long cherished Kurt Lewin's famous formula, $B=f(P,E)$, that behavior is a function of personality and the environment. But what particular aspects of the environment interact with personality in affecting behavior? In order to make sense of the many situational variables which might be crucial to our understanding of leadership effectiveness, we need to go back to a few fundamentals. We know that different types of leaders perform well in different types of situations. But what are the critical differences in the situations which will help us predict leadership effectiveness?

If leadership is indeed a relationship based on power and influence, then it seems reasonable to classify situations on the basis of the power and influence which they give the leader. The liked chairman of a volunteer committee has considerably more power than one who is disliked and rejected. The captain of a ship has more power than the director of a church choir. When the captain gives an order to one of his subordinates, he can be fairly certain that it will be carried out. The committee chairman faces considerably more uncertainty: will his group support him? Will his instructions lead to the solution of the problem? If he expresses his wish to move in one direction rather than another, will the group members agree or resign?

Underlying these questions are two related dimensions of the situation. The first one is the degree to which the situation provides the leader with control and influence, that is, the extent to which the leader is, or feels, able to obtain the outcomes he desires. Closely related to this is the question of predictability. To what extent can the leader predict what will happen when he gives an order, when he opts for one method of attacking the job as against another, when he rewards or disciplines one of his subordinates?

Note that the aspects of the situation with which we are here concerned are quite similar to those which Campbell and his associates (1970) saw as common to organizational climate factors. They spoke of consideration, warmth, and support, of orientation toward rewards and punishments, and of the degree to which the job and the task were structured. How, then, do we measure the control and influence which the situation provides the leader? The success of measuring or classifying the situation must be judged by how well this method enables us to predict leadership performance. A wide variety of methods have been developed to characterize leadership situations. At this point we plan to present the method basic to understanding the leadership effectiveness theory on which this book is based. It involves three components which are described below.

Leader-member relations

From a theoretical as well as an intuitive point of view, the interpersonal relationship between the leader and his group members is likely to be the most important single variable which determines his power and influence. This assumption is also supported by several empirical studies (e.g., Fishbein et al., 1969). The leader's authority depends upon his acceptance by his members. If others are willing to follow him because of his pleasant personality, his trustworthiness, or his charisma, the leader has little need for the organizational support provided by task structure and position power. If the leader is distrusted, his situation will necessarily be less favorable even when organizational support is at his disposal. Very few tasks can be so structured that they cannot be sabotaged or delayed by a disaffected subordinate. Very few supervisors have enough power to coerce a recalcitrant worker or to fire him as long as he performs on a minimally acceptable level.

While the leader's personality undoubtedly affects his relationship with his group members, it is not by any means completely determined by them. The personality of group members plays a part (e.g., Haythorne et al., 1956) which has sometimes been neglected. A person who is replacing a highly successful and admired leader is likely to obtain considerably less support from his group than is one who replaces a despised martinet. Moreover, someone promoted to management from the ranks might or might not have good rapport with his new subordinates. They may consider him one of their own and support him, or they may be jealous of his success.

The leader-member relations dimension has been measured in two ways. One method involves asking the members of the group to indicate on a sociometric preference scale whether they accept or endorse their leader. These questions are rather difficult to ask, and the answers must be regarded with considerable caution. A man who says that he does not regard his supervisor very highly is really laying his career on the line.

Questions of this type have to be carefully formulated so that they will allow subordinates to choose or not to choose their own supervisor without directly compromising themselves. Thus, one might ask, "With which three employees and managers whom you know in this company would you most prefer to work?" or "Suppose you were to be transferred to a new office. Which three people in this company would you most prefer to have with you?" A respondent may thus indicate his lack of enthusiasm for his boss by naming either others from his own group or managers from outside his group.

In our own research, the groups were usually divided into those above and below the median of choices for the leader. Half of the groups were therefore considered to have good leader-member relations, while half were considered to have poor relations. Where sufficient groups were available, we divided the groups into an upper, a middle, and a lower third, in order to obtain a better differentiation between groups with good and poor leader-member relations.

An alternative method for identifying leader-member relations is the short "Group Atmosphere" (GA) scale. This measure consists of ten eight-point bipolar items which can be answered in the space of two or three minutes. The leader is simply asked to describe his work group on this scale. Two sample items are shown here:

Pleasant ____:____:____:____:____:____:____:____ Unpleasant
           8   7   6   5   4   3   2   1
Friendly ____:____:____:____:____:____:____:____ Unfriendly
          8   7   6   5   4   -3   2   1

The other items are Bad—Good; Worthless—Valuable; Distant—Close; Cold—Warm; Quarrelsome—Harmonious; Self-assured—Hesitant; Efficient—Inefficient; and Gloomy—Cheerful.

The item scores are summed and they may be averaged. An analysis by Posthuma (1970) of 2415 subjects shows the median GA score for a ten-item scale for real-life groups to be 64.9 and for laboratory groups 67.0. McNamara (1968) found that the leader's GA score indicates the degree to which the group is loyal and supportive of the leader, even when the group members do not feel that the leader is very efficient. Chemers and Skrzypek (1972) also found a substantial relationship between sociometric preferences expressed by group members and the leader's GA score. However, in some studies the leader's group atmosphere score has been unrelated to the group members' preference ratings. This has been especially true in short-term laboratory studies in which the leader has practically no chance to become well acquainted with his coworkers and in which sociometric preference ratings are unlikely to be meaningful since the leader may be unable to estimate the group members' feelings toward him. In most cases, the group atmosphere score seems to provide a very quick and valid measure of the leader's *feeling* of being accepted which may, of course, affect his behavior much more than the degree of *actual* acceptance by his group.

Task structure

The second most important measure of situational favorableness is the task-structure dimension. The degree to which the task requirements are spelled out determines in large part the leader's authority to give instructions and to evaluate performance. We generally do not think of the task as providing the leader with power and influence. Yet it is clear upon brief reflection that the supervisor who has a manual of operating procedures in his hand, or who follows in step-by-step fashion the organization's requirements for performing a particular task, enjoys the complete backing of the organization. It would be very difficult for an employee to challenge the leader's right to tell him what to do when the leader can point to the manual's detailed operating instructions.

At the other extreme is the task which is completely unstructured and vague. Here the leader usually has no more knowledge than his members, and he therefore enjoys no advantage over them. His own preferences for proceeding with the task are perhaps no more justified than would be those of any other member of the group. If the task consists, for instance, of developing a new policy statement, it is highly unlikely that the leader will have much advantage in expertise. It is even more unlikely that his method of proceeding is on its face more meritorious than that proposed by any other group member as an alternative. The members are therefore quite justified in questioning the leader's approach, even where his formal position power is quite high. As a result, an unstructured task implies correspondingly lower control and influence.

Shaw's (1963, 1971) dimensions of task characteristics, mentioned above, provide a useful means of evaluating the structure of the task. Of the several features of his *solution multiplicity* factor which can be measured, four have been used in our own studies. These are:

1) *Goal clarity.* This is the degree to which the requirements of a job (the tasks and duties which typically make up the job) are clearly stated or known to people performing the job. It would be quite low for such jobs as director of a railroad switching yard or private detective, but quite high for an axle assembler in an auto plant who secures front and rear assemblies to chassis springs.

2) *Goal-path multiplicity.* This is the degree to which the problems encountered in the job can be solved by a variety of procedures (number of different alternatives in performing the job, number of different ways the problems typically encountered in the job can be solved). A job with very low goal-path multiplicity, and hence with high structure, would be that of a date puller, who "cuts open dates, removes the stones, and cuts the dates into pieces for use in making candy." High in this category would be the job of research engineer who "conducts engineering research concerned with processing a particular kind of commodity with a view to improving present products and discovering new products. . . . Plans and executes experimental work to check theories advanced. . . ."

3) *Decision verifiability.* This is the degree to which the "correctness" of the solutions or decisions typically encountered in a job can be demonstrated by appeal to authority or authoritative source (e.g., the census of 1960), by logical procedures (e.g., mathematical demonstration), or by feedback (e.g., examination of the consequences of the decision, as in action tasks). A social welfare research worker's job, which involves "research to facilitate investigation and alleviation of social problems . . ." would be very low on this scale. A nut and bolt sorter who ". . . sorts nuts and bolts by hand according to size, length, and diameter . . . " would be very high.

4) *Decision specificity.* This is the degree to which there is generally more than one "correct solution" involved in tasks which typically make up a job. Some tasks, like arithmetic problems, are high on this dimension since they have only one solution that is acceptable; others have an almost infinite

number of possible solutions, all of which may be equally good. Examples might be human relations problems or problems about which managers must make decisions. Low on this scale, and hence low in task structure, would again be a social welfare research worker's job. Very high would be the job of a barrel drainer who "empties water from barrel that has been inspected or weighed by rolling barrel onto a stand and pulling bung from hole by hand."

In our research, we have generally had each of the four dimensions scored by judges on a scale from 1 (low structure) to 8 (high structure). Groups above the median (a score of 5.0) are generally considered to have high task structure and those below the median to have low structure. Hunt (1967) has developed a more extensive scaling procedure (see the Appendix), which is particularly useful for studies of ongoing organizations.

Position power

As we have discussed before, the most obvious way in which we vest power in the leader (though not the most important) is by giving him the right to direct, evaluate, and reward and punish those he is asked to supervise, though these legitimate aspects of his job can be exercised only within rather strictly defined boundaries. In most situations, the subordinates have a very clear idea of the leader's legitimate authority, and only rarely is this authority seriously challenged.

The scale which we have found useful in determining leader position power in business organizations is a simple check list also devised by Hunt (1967). Each of the items can be answered yes or no.

1) Can the supervisor recommend subordinate rewards and punishments to his boss?

2) Can the supervisor punish or reward subordinates on his own?

3) Can the supervisor recommend promotion or demotion of subordinates?

4) Does the supervisor's special knowledge allow him to decide how subordinates are to proceed on their jobs?

5) Can the supervisor promote or demote subordinates on his own?

6) Can the supervisor specifically instruct subordinates concerning what they are to do?

7) Is it an important part of the supervisor's job to motivate his subordinates?

8) Is it an important part of the supervisor's job to evaluate subordinate performance?

9) Does the supervisor have a great deal of knowledge about the jobs under him but require his subordinates to do them?

10) Can the supervisor supervise and evaluate subordinate jobs?

11) Does the supervisor know both his own and his subordinates' jobs so that he could finish subordinate work himself if it were necessary and he had enough time?

12) Has the supervisor been given an official title by the company which differentiates him from subordinates?

While these checklists are quite helpful in operationally defining high or low position power, it is in fact only rarely necessary to rate leadership positions in work contexts. Practically all managers, supervisors, foremen, and superintendents in business and industry have high position power. Practically all committee chairmen and leaders of groups of colleagues tend to have low position power. The scales are needed mostly for those cases in which there is an unusual leadership situation.

SITUATIONAL FAVORABLENESS

The three aspects of the situation which appear to be of most importance in determining the leader's control and influence appear to be (1) whether the leader's group atmosphere score, or the sociometric preference for the leader, is high or low; (2) whether the task is relatively structured or unstructured; and (3) whether the position power is relatively high or low. A particular group may be classified by first ordering it on leader-member relations, then on task structure, and finally on position power. A group may then be placed in one of eight conceptual cells, ranging from the most favorable one, in which leader-member relations, task structure, and position power are all high, to the least favorable, in which all three values are low. The resulting classification is shown in Figure 4–1.

FIGURE 4–1.   The Situational Favorableness Dimension.

	I	II	III	IV	V	VI	VII	VIII
Leader-member Relations	Good				Poor			
Task Structure	High		Low		High		Low	
Position Power	Strong	Weak	Strong	Weak	Strong	Weak	Strong	Weak

This definition of situational favorableness is not without its problems or its critics. It is at best a rough index, which, we hope, will eventually become more precise. We must develop new methods for measuring favorableness in absolute rather than relative terms, that is, for determining not only whether one situation is higher or lower in task structure, but also by how much it is higher or lower. We must also find ways of taking into account the possibility that position power in some organizations, such as a marine recruit unit, may be much more important than the leader's relationship with his members, or that task structure in a highly programmed operation like a countdown procedure may be the single most important aspect of that situation.

There is also evidence that other aspects of the situation might play an important part. These include the motivation, intelligence, training, and experience of leaders and group members, as well as such extra-organizational factors as the community's economic situation. Which of these will have to be included in future studies of more complex leadership problems is a question for further research.

Having said all this, it is nevertheless true that the situational favorableness dimension is a very useful empirical and theoretical tool which has contributed a great deal to our understanding of leadership performance and leadership behavior. It is the tool upon which the remaining chapters of this book are based.

REFERENCES

Barnard, C. *The Functions of the Executive.* Harvard University Press, 1938.

Blau, P. M., and W. R. Scott. *Formal Organizations: A Comparative Approach.* Chandler, 1962.

Brayfield, A. H., and W. H. Crockett. "Employee attitudes and employee performance." *Psychological Bulletin* 52 (1955): 396–429.

Burns, T., and G. M. Stalker. *The Management of Innovation.* Quadrangle, 1961.

Campbell, J. P., M. D. Dunnette, E. E. Lawler, III, and K. E. Weick. *Managerial Behavior, Performance, and Effectiveness.* McGraw-Hill, 1970.

Chemers, M. M., and G. J. Skrzypek. "An experimental test of the Contingency Model of leadership effectiveness." *Journal of Personality and Social Psychology* 24 (1972): 172–77.

Csoka, L. S. "Intelligence: A critical variable for leadership experience." Technical Report No. 72–34. Organizational Research Group, University of Washington, 1972.

Fiedler, F. E. "The effect of leadership and cultural heterogeneity on group performance: A test of the Contingency Model." *Journal of Experimental Social Psychology* 2 (1966): 237–64.

Fiedler, F. E. *A Theory of Leadership Effectiveness.* McGraw-Hill, 1967.

Filley, A. C., and R. J. House. *Managerial Process and Organizational Behavior.* Scott, Foresman and Company, 1969.

Fishbein, M., E. Landy, and G. Hatch. "Consideration of two assumptions underlying Fiedler's Contingency Model for the prediction of leadership effectiveness." *American Journal of Psychology* 4 (1969): 457–73.

French, J. R. P., Jr., and B. H. Raven. "The bases of social power." In *Studies in Social Power,* D. Cartwright, ed., pp. 118–49. University of Michigan Press, 1959.

Hackman, J. R. "Toward understanding the role of tasks in behavior research." *Acta Psychologica* 39 (1969): 97–128.

Harsanyi, J. C. "Measurement of social power, opportunity costs, and the theory of two-person bargaining games." *Behavioral Science* 7 (1962): 67–80.

Haythorn, W., A. Couch, D. Haefner, P. Langhan, and L. Carter. "The effects of varying combinations of authoritarian and equalitarian leaders and followers." *Journal of Abnormal and Social Psychology* 53 (1956): 210–19.

Hunt, J. G. "Fiedler's leadership contingency model: An empirical test in three organizations." *Organizational Behavior and Human Performance* 2 (1967): 290–308.

Jacobs, T. O. *Leadership and Exchange in Formal Organizations.* Human Resources Research Organization, 1970.

McGrath, J. E., and I. Altman. *Small Group Research*. Holt, Rinehart & Winston, 1966.

McNamara, V. D. "Leadership, staff, and school effectiveness." Unpublished doctoral dissertation, University of Alberta, 1968.

Morris, C. G., II. "Effects of task characteristics on group process." Technical Report No. 2. AFDSR Contract AF 49(638)–1291, University of Illinois, Urbana, 1965. .

Peabody, R. L. "Perceptions of organizational authority: A comparative analysis." *Administrative Science Quarterly* 6 (1962): 463–82.

Posthuma, A. B. "Normative data on the least preferred co-worker scale (LPC) and the group atmosphere questionnaire (GA)." Organizational Research, University of Washington, 1970.

Raven, B. "Power and leadership." In *Current Studies in Social Psychology*, I. D. Steiner and M. Fishbein, eds. Holt, Rinehart & Winston, 1965.

Russell, B. *Power: A New Social Analysis*. Allen & Unwin, 1938.

Shaw, M. E. "Scaling group tasks: A method for dimensional analysis." Technical Report No. 1. University of Florida, 1963.

Shaw, M. E. *Group Dynamics: The Psychology of Group Behavior*. McGraw-Hill, 1971.

Schneider, B., and C. J. Bartlett. "Individual differences and organizational climate: The research plan and questionnaire development." *Personnel Psychology* 21 (1968): 323–34.

Tannenbaum, A. S. *Control in Organizations*. McGraw-Hill, 1968.

Woodward, J. *Industrial Organization: Theory and Practice*. Oxford University Press, 1965.

What Makes Groups Effective?

5

As we have seen in previous chapters, no single personality trait, trait pattern, or particular style of leader behavior assures good organizational performance in all leadership situations. A person may be a very effective leader in one situation but very ineffective in another. A number of recent theories of leadership have therefore investigated the particular conditions under which one or another type of leadership behavior or leader personality is most effective.

The best articulated theory of this kind is the *Contingency Model* of leadership effectiveness, according to which the performance of a group is *contingent* upon both the motivational system of the leader and the degree to which the leader has control and influence in a particular situation, the "situational favorableness."

This theory represents a departure from previous thinking. It views the leadership situation as an arena in which the leader seeks to satisfy his own as well as the organization's goals. The degree to which he will be able to do so will, of course, depend upon the control and influence at his disposal.

The personality measure which is the key variable in the contingency theory is the so-called Least Preferred Coworker (LPC) score. It is obtained by asking the individual to think of everybody with whom he has ever worked and to describe the person with whom he could work least well, his "least preferred coworker." Each item of this simple bipolar scale is scored from one to eight, with eight as the most favorable point on the scale, and the LPC score is the sum of the item scores. In most of our work we have used a scale of sixteen items, reproduced in Figure 5–1.

It takes only two or three minutes to complete the scale, and the score is fairly reliable. That is, most people will fill it out consistently on successive tests. They may produce a very negative description (low LPC) or a relatively more positive description (middle or high LPC) of their least preferred coworker, but the LPC scale seems to be about as stable over time as many other personality measures. (We will discuss the consistency of the score in greater detail in Chapter 6.) A low score indicates the degree to which an individual is ready to reject completely those with whom he cannot work, an attitude which is reflected by describing them in negative terms on attributes which are not directly related to their work. A highly rejecting description indicates a very strong emotional reaction and not merely the calm and reasoned judgment of a detached observer. A more positive score indicates a willingness to perceive even the worst coworker as having some reasonably positive attributes and again reflects more than a simple objective judgment. The high LPC person who sees both good and bad points in his least preferred coworker takes a much more analytical point of view which suggests a greater concern with knowing even those with whom he cannot work.

WHAT DOES THE LPC SCORE MEASURE?

Despite the simplicity of the LPC score and the way we obtain it, the road to understanding LPC has been a maddening and frustrating odyssey. For nearly 20 years, we have been attempting to correlate it with every conceivable personality trait and every conceivable behavior observation score. By and large these analyses have been uniformly fruitless. In fact, for many years we despaired of finding any relationship at all between LPC and personality test scores. At the same time, it was quite obvious that this score must measure a very important personality variable since the correlations between LPC and group performance were quite high and significant. We knew that we were on to something, but not until quite recently were we able to specify more exactly what this might be.

It now appears that LPC is an index of a motivational hierarchy, or of behavioral preferences, implying that some goals are more important to the individual than others. That such hierarchies

FIGURE 5-1. Think of the Person with Whom You Can Work Least Well. He May Be Someone You Work with Now, or He May Be Someone You Knew in the Past. He Does Not Have to Be the Person You Like Least Well, But Should Be the Person with Whom You Had the Most Difficulty in Getting a Job Done. Describe This Person as He Appears to You. Source: Fiedler, 1967, p. 41. Reprinted by permission of McGraw-Hill.

Pleasant	__ :	__ :	__ :	__ :	__ :	__ :	__ :	__	Unpleasant
	8	7	6	5	4	3	2	1	
Friendly	__ :	__ :	__ :	__ :	__ :	__ :	__ :	__	Unfriendly
	8	7	6	5	4	3	2	1	
Rejecting	__ :	__ :	__ :	__ :	__ :	__ :	__ :	__	Accepting
	1	2	3	4	5	6	7	8	
Helpful	__ :	__ :	__ :	__ :	__ :	__ :	__ :	__	Frustrating
	8	7	6	5	4	3	2	1	
Unenthusiastic	__ :	__ :	__ :	__ :	__ :	__ :	__ :	__	Enthusiastic
	1	2	3	4	5	6	7	8	
Tense	__ :	__ :	__ :	__ :	__ :	__ :	__ :	__	Relaxed
	1	2	3	4	5	6	7	8	
Distant	__ :	__ :	__ :	__ :	__ :	__ :	__ :	__	Close
	1	2	3	4	5	6	7	8	
Cold	__ :	__ :	__ :	__ :	__ :	__ :	__ :	__	Warm
	1	2	3	4	5	6	7	8	
Cooperative	__ :	__ :	__ :	__ :	__ :	__ :	__ :	__	Uncooperative
	8	7	6	5	4	3	2	1	
Supportive	__ :	__ :	__ :	__ :	__ :	__ :	__ :	__	Hostile
	8	7	6	5	4	3	2	1	
Boring	__ :	__ :	__ :	__ :	__ :	__ :	__ :	__	Interesting
	1	2	3	4	5	6	7	8	
Quarrelsome	__ :	__ :	__ :	__ :	__ :	__ :	__ :	__	Harmonious
	1	2	3	4	5	6	7	8	
Self-assured	__ :	__ :	__ :	__ :	__ :	__ :	__ :	__	Hesitant
	8	7	6	5	4	3	2	1	
Efficient	__ :	__ :	__ :	__ :	__ :	__ :	__ :	__	Inefficient
	8	7	6	5	4	3	2	1	
Gloomy	__ :	__ :	__ :	__ :	__ :	__ :	__ :	__	Cheerful
	1	2	3	4	5	6	7	8	
Open	__ :	__ :	__ :	__ :	__ :	__ :	__ :	__	Guarded
	8	7	6	5	4	3	2	1	

exist is a well-known fact of everyday life: If I give each of ten people $100, it is a safe bet that they will spend this money differently. Some will buy food rather than clothes; some will put it into a savings account rather than take a vacation. Likewise, if I tell them that they will have a free day next week, some may decide to sleep, others may want to spend it with their families, and still others may plan to go fishing or sailing. These choice behaviors reflect the hierarchical arrangement of their goals.

Let us assume then that each individual has a hierarchy of goals, that is, that individual A's first priority might be getting through school and his second priority, having a good time. In contrast, individual B's first priority might be having a good time and his second, getting through school. It is now highly probable that the preferred behaviors of A and B will differ. If the time is limited, A will study and forgo dates and parties, while B will go on dates and parties instead of studying. If, on the other hand, there is no time pressure, and A has already done his studying, or feels that it will surely get done, he will go out to have a good time. B, on the other hand, might feel that he will not lose out on having a good time, and he will therefore spend some of his time on his studies. As Maslow (1954) has pointed out, satisfied needs no longer motivate. If I have satisfied my hunger, I will no longer be motivated by more food, and I will then seek to satisfy my less basic goals, the "luxuries" of life.

Let us now return to the leadership situation and the part which LPC plays. Recent research strongly suggests that the high LPC person, who perceives his least preferred coworker in a more favorable, more differentiated manner, has as his basic goal the desire to be "related." That is, he seeks to have strong emotional and affective ties with others in the work situation (and probably in other situations as well).[1] If this basic goal is achieved, if he feels that he has achieved such an affective relationship, he will also seek, as his secondary goals, status and esteem. He will want to be admired and to be recognized (Fiedler, 1972b).

The low LPC person has a different hierarchy of goals. His basic goal is to accomplish the task. His self-esteem is derived from achievement. However, as long as accomplishing the task presents no

1. *It should be pointed out, by the way, that being related need not necessarily mean that the relationship is positive. Many people prefer even a negative or hostile relationship to not being related. Consider, for example, the married couples who continually fight with each other, or the work relations which are characterized by friendly sarcasm and an undertone of hostility.*

problems, why not also have friendly, pleasant relations with the members of the work group? In other words, as long as the low LPC leader knows that the task accomplishment is in the bag, he can afford to be friendly and concerned with the feelings of his coworkers. It is only when task accomplishment is threatened that good interpersonal relations must take second place.

The person who sees even his least preferred coworker in a relatively positive manner (high LPC) tends, somewhat like Mc-Gregor's (1967) Theory Y person, to be more optimistic about human nature and more ready to allow others greater freedom (Nebeker and Hansson, 1973).[2]

LPC AND LEADERSHIP PERFORMANCE

Let us now ask how it will affect a leader's performance if he is primarily motivated to seek close interpersonal relations, or, alternatively, effective task performance. Most books on leadership tacitly assume that the leader will as a matter of course seek to accomplish the organization's goals. Hence, the more power and influence the organization is able to give him, the better he will be able to ensure that the organizational goals will be obtained.

This rather simplistic concept of leadership does not take sufficient account of the fact that human beings have strong needs. While all foremen in a plant are likely to tell us that they want high productivity, they will differ in how this productivity should be achieved, and they will differ in the price they are willing to pay for high productivity. And above all, they will view the job in terms of the particular way it will satisfy their needs.

As we have stressed before, leadership is a relationship based on control and influence. It is obvious that the person with complete control and influence over his own fate and that of others can ensure that all his goals are achieved. Under these favorable conditions he will be able to pursue his secondary goals. Hence, the high LPC

2. Mitchell (1970) and Foa, Mitchell, and Fiedler (1971) have shown that the high LPC person tends to be cognitively more complex and that he differentiates more in his perception and evaluation of his interpersonal environment. This is quite compatible with the interpretation of LPC as an index of a motivational hierarchy. A person who values relationships more is likely to pay more attention to others and to trust them more than someone who is indifferent about his interpersonal relations.

leader will concern himself with such status-enhancing activities as ordering people around, assigning tasks, and assuming responsibility. The low LPC leader, given this high degree of control, will be relaxed, friendly, and considerate, in the knowledge that the task presents no problem.

In the unfavorable situation in which the leader's control is low, where he cannot be sure of his group's support, has little power to coerce his subordinates, and cannot be certain of the way the task should be done, the high LPC leader will seek first of all the anxiety-reducing comfort of the close relationship with his group members. The low LPC leader will try to get the task done even if he has to step on toes and ruffle feathers.

LPC AND GROUP PERFORMANCE

Obviously, the favorableness of the leadership situation makes a big difference in the behavior and performance of the group. In the preceding chapter we discussed a method of classifying situations which was based on three aspects of the situation—acceptance, structure, and power. Each of these three dimensions was divided in half so that any group can be classified high or low on each dimension, yielding an eight-celled classification system.

Let us now see what happens when we classify various types of groups in this way. For each set of groups which falls into one of the eight cells or octants, we can compute a correlation coefficient which tells us the degree to which the leader's LPC score is correlated with the group's performance. If we find that leaders with high LPC scores are more successful, that they have better group performance than do leaders with low LPC scores, the correlation will be positive. If the task-motivated leaders with low LPC scores are more successful than high LPC leaders, the correlation will be negative.[3]

DEVELOPMENT OF THE CONTINGENCY MODEL

The data for the original analyses of LPC and situational variables came from a program of leadership research which was begun

3. *See Footnote 1 of Chapter 2 for a review of the correlation coefficient.*

in 1951 at the University of Illinois. All studies involved interacting groups—groups in which the members had to interact and coordinate their efforts to achieve a common goal—rather than coacting groups. In essence, we have an interacting group when it is impossible to arrive at a group product by simply adding the performance scores of each group member (e.g., a basketball team or a policy-making group). Examples of coacting groups are departments in which employees perform on a piece-work basis or classroom situations in which each student receives an individual grade.

Wherever possible, we used "hard" or objective performance criteria which reflected the major assigned goal of the group. Thus, in a study of high school basketball teams, the criterion of performance consisted of the win/loss ratio of games played in league competition. In a second study of land surveying parties, the criterion was the accuracy of measuring various sections of land, as rated by class instructors. Other studies in the program dealt with B-29 air force combat crews where performance was measured by means of circular error bombing accuracy, tank crews where performance was based on time-in-seconds to hit a target, antiaircraft artillery crews where effectiveness ratings were available, and management and boards of directors of 32 consumer cooperative companies where various profit indices were assessed. Also included were a wide variety of experimentally assembled groups consisting of ROTC students, executives participating in leadership training workshops, and students who had to take part in research as one of the requirements for a course. Well over 800 groups were studied between 1951 and 1963, and the theory was based on the findings of these various studies.

The averaged results of the various analyses are plotted in Figure 5–2. The horizontal axis of this graph indicates the favorableness of the situation with the most favorable cell or octant shown on the far left and the least favorable cell on the far right. The vertical axis indicates the degree to which the leader's LPC score and his group's performance are correlated in various sets of groups within a cell. A point on the graph above the midline shows a positive correlation between LPC and group performance, that is, it shows that the high LPC leaders performed better than did the low LPC leaders. A point below the midline shows that the low LPC leaders performed better than did the high LPC leaders, that the correlation was negative. The heavy line connects the median correlation coefficients and indicates the most likely value of the correlation coefficient in each of the eight cells—in other words, the best prediction for the correlations.

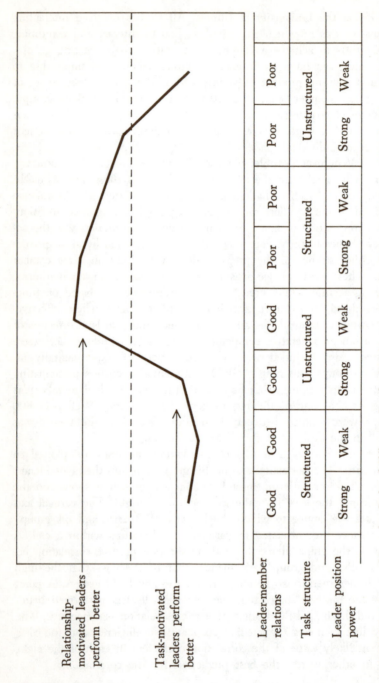

Leader-member relations	Good	Good	Good	Good	Poor	Poor	Poor	Poor
Task structure	Structured		Unstructured		Structured		Unstructured	
Leader position power	Strong	Weak	Strong	Weak	Strong	Weak	Strong	Weak

FIGURE 5–2.   How the Style of Effective Leadership Varies with the Situation. Source: Modified from Fiedler, 1965, with the permission of the *Harvard Business Review*.

As Figure 5–2 shows, the task-motivated (low LPC) leaders performed most effectively in the very favorable situations of octants I, II, and III, and in the relatively unfavorable situations, such as octant VIII. Hence, we obtain negative correlations between LPC and group performance scores. Relationship-motivated (high LPC) leaders obtain optimal group performance under situations of moderate or intermediate favorableness (octants IV and V). These are situations in which (A) the task is structured but the leader is disliked and must, presumably, be diplomatic and concerned with the feeling of his men, or (B) the liked leader has an unstructured task and must therefore depend upon the creativity and willing participation of his members.

The Contingency Model leads to the major hypothesis that leadership effectiveness depends upon the leader's style of interacting with his group members and the favorableness of the group-task situation. Specifically, low LPC leaders who are primarily task-motivated perform best under conditions that are very favorable or very unfavorable for them. Relationship-motivated leaders perform best under conditions that are of moderate favorableness.

HOW VALID IS THE CONTINGENCY MODEL?

A theory based on existing data is necessarily suspect. The critical test of any theory is the degree to which it permits us to predict future outcomes. Over thirty different studies have now been conducted to test the predictions of the Contingency Model. These studies are reviewed in detail elsewhere (Fiedler, 1971a) and will be summarized only briefly at this point.

In all of the validation studies represented in Table 5–1, the groups were classified as high or low on leader-member relations, task structure, and position power, which placed them in one of the eight octants. In groups falling into the same octant, the leader's LPC score was correlated with the criterion of group or organizational performance. Where possible, these criterion scores were based on objective measures; otherwise the performance was evaluated by judges or by ratings of superiors. The hypothesis of the validation studies was that the task-motivated leaders would perform better than relationship motivated leaders in octants I, II, and III as well as in VIII or still less favorable situations. The relationship-motivated leaders would perform best

TABLE 5–1.   Summary of Field and Laboratory Studies Testing the Contingency Model. Source: Fiedler, 1971a. Copyright 1971 by the American Psychological Association and reproduced by permission.

Field Studies				Octants				
	I	II	III	IV	V	VI	VII	VIII
Hunt (1967)	−.67		−.80		.21		.30	
	−.51						−.30	
Hill (1969)		−.10	−.29			−.24	.62	
Fiedler et al. (1969)		−.21		.00		.67 *		−.51
O'Brien and Fiedler (unpublished)		−.46		.47		−.45		−.14
Tumes (1972)	−.47			.62**				
Laboratory Experiments								
Belgian Navy								
(Fiedler, 1966)	−.72	.37	−.16	.08	.16	.07	.26	−.37
	−.77	.50	−.54	.13	.03	.14	−.27	.60
Shima (1968)		−.26		.71*				
Mitchell (1969)		.24		.43				
		.17		.38				
Fiedler Exec.		.34		.51				
Chemers and Skrzy-								
pek (1972)	−.43	−.32	.10	.35	.28	.13	.08	−.33
Rice and Chemers								
(1973)						.30		−.40
Sashkin (1972)			−.29					
Median, all studies	−.59	.17	−.29	.40	.22	.13	.26	−.35
Median, field studies	−.51	−.21	−.29	.47	.21	−.24	.30	−.33
Median, laboratory experiments	−.72	.24	−.16	.38	.16	.13	.08	−.37
Medians in original studies	−.52	−.58	−.33	.47	.42		.05	−.43

Number of correlations in the expected direction: 38 [1]
Number of correlations opposite to expected direction: 9
p by biomial test: .01
    [1] exclusive of octant VI, for which no prediction had been made.
    * $p < .05$
  ** $p < .01$

in octants IV and V and perhaps in VI and VII, that is, in the moderately favorable situations. Since high LPC indicates relationship motivation, the correlation coefficients should be negative in octants I, II, III, and VIII and positive in octants IV and V, and perhaps in VI and VII.

A fairly detailed review of all the validation studies can be found in a paper by Fiedler (1972a). For the purposes of this book, it may be enough to say that these studies included a very wide variety of teams and organizations, e.g., navy teams, chemical research teams, shop departments, supermarkets, heavy machinery plant departments, engineering groups, hospital wards, public health teams, and others.

It is quite clear from the results (shown in Figure 5–3) that the theory is highly predictive and that the relations obtained in the validation studies are almost identical to those obtained in the original studies. With the exception of octant II, the median correlations match almost exactly. The Model predicts negative correlations while the studies conducted in laboratories—but not under field conditions—obtained positive correlations between LPC and performance. This might mean that the Model is wrong or that octant II is difficult to build into a laboratory experiment. This octant includes groups with a liked leader and a structured task, but low position power—a situation which, in fact, does not occur very frequently in real life.

We are of the opinion that the Model is more likely to be correct than the laboratory studies. We base this judgment on the findings from field studies which show negative correlations, as well as from a large field experiment at West Point which, because of its importance to the theory, will be described here more fully.

MILITARY CADET GROUPS

One of the criticisms that has been leveled at the Contingency Model is that the leader-member relations have usually been determined at the conclusion of the study, and that the success of the group could, therefore, influence them. It has also been charged that the theory has never been completely tested (e.g., Ashour, 1973) and that the situational favorableness has not been sufficiently defined in advance. These criticisms were met by a large experiment conducted at the United States Military Academy at West Point by Chemers and Skrzypek (1972). This field experiment tested all eight situations on octants of the Contingency Model exactly as they are specified and with strong manipulation of variables. The subjects in this experiment were 128 first-year cadets attending summer camp maneuvers at the Military Academy.

All cadets were given the LPC scale as well as a sociometric test to indicate their most and least preferred fellow cadets. These

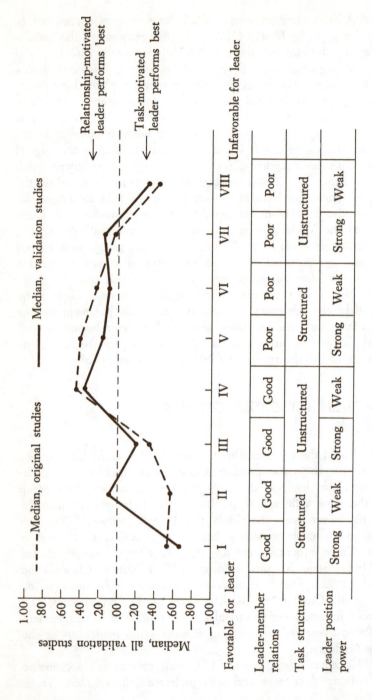

FIGURE 5–3.   Correlations Between Leader LPC Scores and Performance in Various Cells of the Situational Favorableness Dimension. Source: Fiedler, F. E., *Leadership*, p. 14, Morristown, N.J.; General Learning Press. © 1971 General Learning Corporation.

preference scores were obtained several weeks before the experiment was conducted. Leaders in half the four-man groups were then assigned to members who had expressed liking for them on the test. In the other half of the groups, leaders were assigned to members who had previously expressed negative feelings and judgments about them.

Two levels of task structure were employed. The unstructured task consisted of writing a proposal to encourage overseas-based enlisted men to become interested in world politics. The highly structured task required the group to make a drawing of a barracks building from a set of detailed specifications. The leader's power was manipulated by giving half the leaders the responsibility of rating the other group members. These ratings would ostensibly be placed in the permanent military record of each man, a very important aspect of his career. The other half of the leaders were described to their groups as chairmen and coordinators without any real power to reward or punish. These three variables yielded the eight-cell favorableness dimension. LPC and group effectiveness were correlated for each octant. The resultant pattern of correlations is shown superimposed over the curve predicted by the Contingency Model in Figure 5–4.

The correspondence between the two curves is striking. The correlation of the points in the two curves is 0.86. This experiment provides very strong support for the Contingency Model as a whole. It also yields a negative, albeit low, correlation between LPC and group performance in octant II, suggesting that the octant II condition is difficult to reproduce in the laboratory but can be produced in a well-designed field experiment with strong manipulation of the variables.

The bottom lines of Table 5–1 summarize the results which have been obtained in appropriately conducted validation studies. The median correlations of the original studies are almost identical to the medians of subsequent validation studies. The correlation between the medians of the original studies and the medians of the validation studies in field, laboratory, and both types of studies are, respectively, 0.85, 0.64, and 0.80 (the first and third are statistically significant). The correlation between the West Point results and the original medians was 0.86, which is significant at the 0.01 level. Moreover, 37 of the correlations in Table 5–1 were in the expected direction and only 11 were in the opposite direction. This is, again, a finding which is statistically highly significant. The joint probability of these findings, using Fisher's exact test, is less than 0.05.

A number of studies have been conducted which followed modified methods for measuring the situational favorableness dimen-

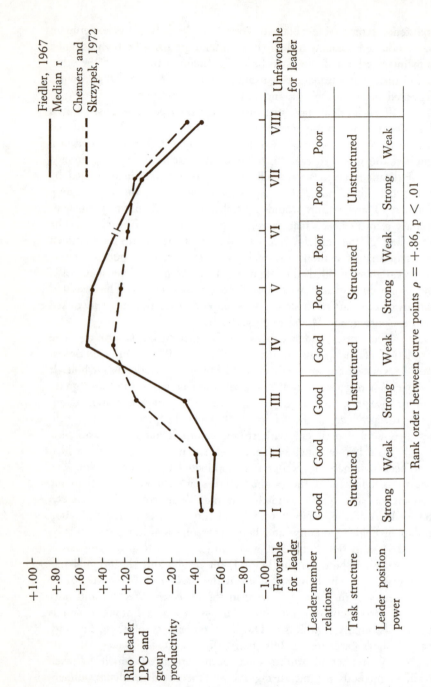

FIGURE 5–4.   Comparison of Predicted and Obtained Curves for LPC and Group Effectiveness. Source: Chemers and Skrzypek, 1972. Copyright 1972 by the American Psychological Association and reproduced by permission.

sion. Some studies differed in amount of stress, some differed in the degree to which the tasks were conducive to leader influence, while still others permitted only a rough classification into high, moderate, or low favorableness. By and large, the correlations followed the predictions of the Model. The median correlations in the favorable and unfavorable situations were −0.37 and −0.30 respectively, while the median in the intermediate situation was 0.30.

By far the strongest evidence in support of a theory comes from its ability to explain previously puzzling findings and from its ability to predict "counterintuitive" results, that is, relationships which are contrary to commonsense expectations. As we shall see in Chapter 8, the Contingency Model correctly predicts under which conditions leadership training and experience will be detrimental to performance.

In general, it seems quite clear that the Contingency Model has considerable validity. The data strongly support the notion that task-motivated leaders perform best in very favorable and in unfavorable situations, while relationship-motivated leaders perform best in moderately favorable situations. These relations are quite substantial in many studies and, considering all the other complexities of the situation which are not included in determining situational favorableness, the magnitude of the typical relationships is rather remarkable.

COACTING GROUPS

A large number of groups and organizations are *coacting* groups, whose tasks, as we indicated earlier, involve virtually independent performances by the group members, even though there might be some aggregate team score. Thus, in a bowling team the score depends on the summation of individual scores by the team members.

Several studies of such groups have been conducted, though they were at first difficult to interpret in the light of the Contingency Model. A recent analysis of the findings suggests that we must separate task groups, which are assembled for the benefit of the organization, and training groups, which exist for the purpose of increasing the ability or competence of the individual trainee.

Task groups

Recent analyses suggest that coacting *task* groups follow the same rules as interacting task groups. These include craft shops in

TABLE 5–2.   Correlational Summary of Studies Extending the Contingency Model to Coacting Task and Training Groups. Source: Fiedler, 1971a. Copyright 1971 by the American Psychological Association and reproduced by permission.

Group	Octants							
	I	II	III	IV	V	VI	VII	VIII
Task groups								
Craft shops	−.48				.90[a]			
Groceries	−.06				.49			
Hospital departments [a]	−.21		−.32		.52		.87	
Telephone offices	−.77				.75			
School principals [a]	−.48				.31			
Median	−.48		−.32		.52		.87	
Training groups								
Naval aviation								
Chief instructors	.45							
	.17							
Informal leaders			.55					
			.28					
Management trainees [a]								
Head instructors	.56					−.20		
Informal leaders	.45		.45					
Student nurses [a]			.63					
Medians	.45		.50			−.20		

[a] Studies not conducted by writer or his associates.

Hunt's (1967) study of a physical laboratory, as well as meat and grocery departments of a chain of supermarkets; Hill's (1969) study of various departments in a hospital; a study of telephone offices in two cities (Bates, 1967); and a study of elementary school principals (McNamara, 1968). Table 5–2 summarizes the results. These indicate, at least in octant I, that low LPC leaders perform more effectively than do high LPC leaders, and in octant V, that high LPC leaders perform more effectively than low LPC leaders. The data for other octants are insufficient for drawing firm conclusions. The results obtained in octants I and V are, of course, similar to those obtained for interacting groups.

Training groups

Our discussion up to now has been devoted to groups and organizations which perform tasks assigned by the organization to achieve organizational goals. However, a substantial number of groups exist expressly for the purpose of assisting an individual to achieve his own goals, that is, to understand himself better, to become more proficient, or to learn human relations or technical skills. These groups may well require a different type of leadership. While we can not offer more than tentative conclusions at this time, groups of this type seem to perform best under relationship-motivated (high LPC) leaders. This conclusion, based on the results of several studies, seems intuitively plausible since we generally assume that an individual is most likely to learn in a permissive and nonthreatening atmosphere.

SUMMARY AND SOME IMPLICATIONS

In this chapter, we have presented a rather complex theory of leadership which holds that both the task-motivated and the relationship-motivated leaders perform well, but under different conditions. The task-motivated leaders perform best in situations in which their power and influence are very high, as well as in situations in which their power and influence are quite low, in which they are under stress, and in which the task, their position power, and the support from their group are uncertain. High LPC leaders perform best in situations in which their power and influence are moderate.

The Contingency Model is today one of our best validated leadership theories. Not only is it based on a host of empirical data from a wide variety of groups and organizations, but it is also supported by subsequent validations in different groups and organizations, though not every study yields the expected answers. This theory, like any other, is a tool, a beginning, rather than an end to our understanding of leadership effectiveness; and we shall examine other aspects of the problem in the succeeding chapters.

One important question is how well this theory accords with everyday life. While a theory need not be obvious, it should certainly not contradict all the experiences which we encounter and observe. Most of the findings and predictions of the Contingency Model do, in fact, fit rather well with our everyday experiences. For example, we know that many people who make an outstanding record as managers at the first or the second level of an organization may become failures at higher levels. The Contingency Model suggests that this might indicate not a lack of intellectual ability but rather the change in leader-

ship situation to one in which the individual is no longer able to function at his best. The gallant young officer who bravely leads his men
up the hill in the face of strong enemy fire may simply not operate
well as the head of a committee or a staff group. The young executive
who has been an outstanding assistant to the vice-president may fail
when he becomes the manager of a plant or of an advertising department.

We also know that certain conditions call for clear directions
and orders rather than participative management. The captain of an
airliner has no business consulting his crew members during the final
approach in a dense landing pattern. Likewise, the chairman of a committee is very likely to fail if he forcefully states his position and
proceeds to pressure his committee members into agreeing with him.
Similarly, when the situation is confused, when the leader has little
power, and when he is disliked, he would be better off paying attention
to the task than waiting until he can develop better interpersonal relations with his group. Under these conditions, unless the leader takes
command of the group and the task assignments, his team is likely to
fall apart. This philosophy is reflected in an old army adage: In an
emergency any orders are better than no orders.

The interaction between appropriate leadership and the group-task
situation is also apparent whenever a major change in an organization
disrupts the structure of the task. Such changes are quite common in
business organizations during a crisis. By definition, a crisis implies a
situation that does not provide ordinary guidelines for behavior. The
man who charges ahead without knowing where he is going only rarely
succeeds. A common response under these circumstances is for the
manager to call his assistants together for consultation. After the crisis
has passed, the organization generally returns to its routine and fairly
well-structured tasks which again require task-oriented leadership.

The opposite situation exists in such organizations as research
and development groups. Here the task begins in a very unstructured
manner. The research director and his assistants typically plan, discuss,
consult, and weigh various approaches. This situation requires a high
degree of permissiveness. However, during the data collection phase—
a highly structured activity in which no deviation or "creativity" is permitted—the research director is likely to become very authoritarian and
directive. After the data have been analyzed there is again room for
discussion about their interpretation, and the leader's behavior again
tends to be more permissive, considerate, and human-relations-oriented
(Sample and Wilson, 1965). The extent to which a leader is capable

of changing his behavior at will is a question which we will take up in the next chapter.

While we will discuss the practical applications of the theory in detail in the chapters which follow, one very important implication should be stressed now. Everything points to the conclusion that there is no such thing as an ideal leader. Task-motivated as well as relationship-motivated leaders excel in some situations and not in others. Hence, everyone who is motivated to seek a leadership role, and everyone who is placed in a leadership role, may be effective provided we place him into a situation which matches his leadership style. The theory allows us to predict what the characteristics of the appropriate situation are. This is the most important single implication of this chapter.

Now that we have been able to describe a theory of leadership, the next steps require us to look at the behavior of leaders with different motivational patterns, the implications of the theory for leadership training, and the improvement of organizational effectiveness. Ultimately, we can analyze the ways organizational design might be improved in the light of the Contingency Model.

REFERENCES

Ashour, A. S. "The Contingency Model of leadership effectiveness: An evaluation." *Organizational Behavior and Human Performance* (1973), in press.

Bates, P. A. "Leadership performance at two managerial levels in the telephone company." Unpublished bachelor's thesis, University of Illinois, 1967.

Chemers, M. M., and G. J. Skrzypek. "An experimental test of the Contingency Model of leadership effectiveness." *Journal of Personality and Social Psychology* 24 (1972): 172–77.

Fiedler, F. E. "Change the job to fit the manager." *Harvard Business Review* 43 (1965): 115–22.

Fiedler, F. E. "The effect of leadership and cultural heterogeneity on group performance: A test of the Contingency Model." *Journal of Experimental Social Psychology* 2 (1966): 237–64.

Fiedler, F. E. *A Theory of Leadership Effectiveness.* McGraw-Hill, 1967.

Fiedler, F. E. "Validation and extension of the contingency model of leadership effectiveness: A review of empirical findings." *Psychological Bulletin* 76 (1971a): 128–48.

Fiedler, F. E. *Leadership.* General Learning Press, 1971b.

Fiedler, F. E. "Personality, motivational systems, and behavior of high and low LPC persons." *Human Relations* 25 (1972a): 391–412.

Fiedler, F. E. "Predicting the effects of leadership training and experience from the Contingency Model." *Journal of Applied Psychology* 56 (1972b): 114–19.

Fiedler, F. E., G. E. O'Brien, and D. R. Ilgen. "The effect of leadership style upon the performance and adjustment of volunteer teams operating in a stressful environment." *Human Relations* 22 (1969): 503–14.

Foa, U. G., T. R. Mitchell, and F. E. Fiedler. "Differentiation matching." *Behavioral Science* 16 (1971): 130–42.

Hill, W. "The validation and extension of Fiedler's theory of leadership effectiveness." *Academy of Management Journal* (March 1969): 33–47.

Hunt, J. G. "Fiedler's leadership Contingency Model: An empirical test in three organizations." *Organizational Behavior and Human Performance* 2 (1967): 290–308.

McGregor, D. *The Professional Manager.* McGraw-Hill, 1967.

McNamara, V. D. "Leadership, staff, and school effectiveness." Unpublished doctoral dissertation, University of Alberta, 1968.

Maslow, A. H. *Motivation and Personality.* Harper & Row, 1954.

Mitchell, T. R. "Leader complexity, leadership style, and group performance." Unpublished doctoral dissertation, University of Illinois, Urbana, 1969.

Mitchell, T. R. "Cognitive complexity and leadership style." *Journal of Personality and Social Psychology* 16 (1970): 166–73.

Nebeker, D. M., and R. O. Hansson. "Confidence in human nature and leader style." Paper presented at the Western Psychological Association Meetings, April 11–14, 1973.

Rice, R. W., and M. M. Chemers. "Predicting leadership emergence using Fiedler's Contingency Model of leadership effectiveness." *Journal of Applied Psychology* (1973), in press.

Sample, J. A., and T. R. Wilson. "Leader behavior, group productivity, and rating of least preferred co-worker." *Journal of Personality and Social Psychology* 13 (1965): 266–70.

Sashkin, M. "Leadership style and group decision effectiveness: Correlational and behavioral tests of Fiedler's Contingency Model." *Organizational Behavior and Human Performance* 8 (1972): 347–62.

Shima, H. "The relationships between the leader's modes of interpersonal cognition and the performance of the group." *Japanese Psychological Research* 10 (1968): 13–30.

Tumes, J. "The Contingency Theory of Leadership: A behavioral investigation." Paper presented at the Eastern Academy of Management Meetings, Boston, Mass., May 5, 1972.

Leader Motivation and Leader Behavior

6

Chapter 5 shows that the leader's Least Preferred Coworker score is the critical personality variable in the Contingency Model. Once we know the favorableness of the leader's situation, this score permits us to predict the group's performance in given situations with a surprisingly high degree of accuracy, especially in view of the many other factors which can affect the performance of a group. These other variables include the leader's and the members' intelligence, task-related abilities, training, experience, motivation, and the leader's relations with his own superiors.

It seems clear that the LPC score must measure a very important personality variable, though there are many reasons why the performances of some groups are better than the performances of others. Each reason, each variable, will account for a portion of the variation, but an average correlation between LPC and group performance of 0.50 tells us that roughly 25 percent of the variation is accounted for by the leader's LPC score. This percentage is particularly impressive when we consider the complexity of the leadership problem, but because we cannot apply theories blindly to problems in real life, it is essential that we understand exactly what the score measures.

Leaders affect group performance by means of verbal or gestural behavior which communicates the leader's directions, evaluations, and attitudes to the group members. Many recent leadership theories have therefore attempted to relate leader behavior directly to group performance. They have tried to show that certain types of behavior are conducive and others are detrimental to effective group performance,

94

on the assumption that this will then permit us to teach leaders how to behave in a way which will ensure effective group performance.

These theories have held, for example, that considerate (human relations-oriented) leader behavior is found in effective groups (Stogdill and Coons, 1957), that effective leaders invite member participation in the planning and decision-making process (Likert, 1961), and that effective leaders in some instances need to be structuring in their approach to directing the group.

By and large, however, the results of such studies have been disappointing. Reviews of the literature (e.g., Korman, 1968; Campbell et al., 1970) have shown that the considerate leader or the structuring leader is not consistently more effective, and that participative management has been effective in some situations (e.g., Coch and French, 1948) but not in others (e.g., Vroom, 1960; Morse and Reimer, 1956). Above all, studies of leader behavior provide only concurrent rather than predictive evidence that a particular leader behavior is associated with group effectiveness. In other words, the research has usually examined an ongoing group and ascertained the relationship between some measure of leader behavior and a measure of group productivity. Such studies do not tell us whether the leader's behavior caused the productivity or whether the leader's behavior was, in fact, affected by the performance of his group. There have been, to our knowledge, no studies where leader behavior, measured in one set of groups and under one set of conditions, has been correlated with group performance in other groups and under other conditions.

Everyday experience tells us that an individual's behavior differs from one situation to another. The same individual will say and do different things in his roles as chairman of a club's board of directors, as coach of a little league team, and as manager of a production department. He will behave differently when his production is comfortably above the standard from when his department is far behind schedule. To give a more specific instance, Nealey and Blood (1968) found that the effective nursing supervisors at the first level of management were described as structuring while the effective supervisors at the second management level were described as nonstructuring.

It is obviously of limited usefulness to know simply that the effective leaders in one situation are considerate, employee-centered, or job-centered, unless the behavior of these leaders will remain constant over different situations or unless the leader's behavior is under his voluntary control. As we shall see, there is little doubt that leader behaviors do change from one situation to another, and there is considerable reason to question just how much control the leader has over his own tendency to behave in one way or another. These are two of the most critical issues in the leadership area. Let us consider each of them briefly.

WHAT DETERMINES
LEADER BEHAVIOR?

Common sense tells us that our behavior is determined both by our voluntary intent to act in a certain fashion and by factors which are to a greater or lesser extent beyond our control. An example of the former is the decision to go to a movie; an extreme example of the latter is an eyeblink in response to a sudden light flash. Most of our social and interpersonal behaviors are, however, more difficult to classify. While we like to believe that we can decide most of the time how we behave, we frequently don't succeed in behaving as we think we should. Consider, for example, the parent who loses his temper with his child even though he knows he should control himself, or the foreman who knows that he should calmly take an insubordinate employee to the appropriate disciplinary committee rather than "blow his stack." Obviously, we do not always do what we know to be the best thing.

The question is not whether people behave as they want to behave, but rather under what conditions they do what they want to do, and under what conditions the influence of situation on personality is the primary determinant of behavior. While this is neither the time nor the place to reopen the ancient controversy between free will and determinism, this issue poses an extremely important practical as well as theoretical question for the psychology of leadership. If leader behavior is determined primarily by the individual's "will," then we can easily teach him, or persuade him, to behave in the most effective way. If his behavior is largely determined by the situation, then our efforts to teach him how to behave will be correspondingly less successful.

While the position that an individual's interpersonal behavior is largely outside his control is not very popular among laymen or most psychologists, the problem demands attention and is likely to remain highly controversial. Our data suggest that leader behavior is more strongly determined by the situation than by what the individual would like to do or thinks he ought to do.

In one recent study (unpublished), we asked seasoned school administrators to indicate how they thought they ought to handle a variety of personnel matters. They could be very considerate by showing only disapproval or trying to persuade, or they could be more directive by making new rules or disciplining the offending individual. We then assigned these same school administrators to leadership positions in small experimentally assembled groups and obtained behavior observations from group members and observers. Thus, the same individuals were asked how they should behave and were then observed in two different situations to determine how they actually behaved.

The results of this study indicated that the behavior of these experienced administrators varied considerably more with the characteristics of the situation than with either the way they felt they should behave or the way they expressly intended to behave.

Thus, while there were some who said that they would only show disapproval as a means of dealing with a variety of personnel problems—a very considerate leader behavior—they in fact were seen as quite inconsiderate by their group members and by the observer. Those who said they would actively discipline were rated as quite considerate in one condition, but as inconsiderate in another condition. Since we must assume that people really intend to behave as they say they do, it appears that the situation must play a substantial role in shaping behavior, while the intent to behave in a certain way plays a lesser part. It is, of course, far too early to close the books on this complicated question, for if these results are supported in subsequent studies, they will require a far-reaching reassessment of our training and behavior theories.

HOW CONSISTENT IS LPC?

Having asked how consistent leader behaviors are over different situations, we must also ask how consistent the LPC score might be. By and large, it is neither as good as one might wish nor as bad as one might fear. First of all, the scale has a very high internal consistency. This means that the person who describes his least preferred coworker negatively on some items will also describe him negatively on other items. The measure for this internal consistency, the split-half reliability, is in the 0.90 to 0.95 range.

The more important question is the test-retest reliability, or stability, of LPC—the consistency of the score over time. It is typically measured by administering identical tests, separated by a time interval, under conditions as nearly identical as possible. As with all personality measures, this consistency depends on a number of factors: the age and maturity of respondents, the length of time between successive tests, and their life experience in that time. In a study of mature faculty members in a nursing school, the retest reliability over a period of 16 to 24 months was 0.67, which is quite high. Other investigators have reported reliabilities as low as 0.30 and as high as 0.90 over short periods of time. A study of army men in various leadership positions during a six-month period involving considerable change in their way of life showed a retest reliability of 0.46; a study of combat crew commanders over a period of two months yielded a correlation of 0.65.

To provide some comparison with other measures, LPC varies considerably less than the typical attitude scales (0.30 to 0.40), and its reliability over time is well within the range of the better personality scales. For example, Robinson and Shaver (1969) report the retest reliability for the Rotter Scale of Internal versus External Control as 0.61 for four weeks and 0.49 for eight weeks, and the Gergen and Morris self-consistency scale as 0.73 over eight weeks.

It is also true, however, that changes in the LPC score occur as a result of changes in an individual's life. E. Drucker (personal communication) found that the LPC scores of army recruits varied more over time when the individual's job was changed from leader to group member, or vice versa, than when his position in the group remained constant. We have also found that a very difficult or stressful interaction in the performance of a laboratory task induces major changes in LPC scores obtained immediately before and after the experimental session. We have reason to believe, however, that these changes in LPC scores are likely to be temporary, perhaps reflecting the individual's reaction to a particular group member who just a few moments ago gave him a hard time. It also appears likely that a successful or unsuccessful leadership experience may affect the individual's LPC score. We have reason to doubt that these changes are permanent and affect the individual's behavior in subsequent leadership situations.

Despite some legitimate questions which must be raised about the stability of LPC scores, the fact remains that the score has predicted group performance over respectable periods of time. Chemers and Skrzypek (1972), for example, obtained LPC scores of leaders three weeks prior to their West Point experiment and obtained LPC-performance correlations, as expected, of above 0.40. Fiedler, O'Brien, and Ilgen (1969) obtained LPC scores from teenagers about four weeks before they were assembled in Honduras to perform volunteer public health work. Team evaluations were not collected until approximately seven to eight weeks afterwards, yet these LPC scores correlated as high as 0.45 and 0.47 with the performance ratings.

RELATIONS OF LPC TO OTHER PERSONALITY MEASURES

We usually interpret a psychological test by correlating it with other, presumably related, tests, or with various behavior observations which are supposed to be related to the test score. That is, to find out whether a particular score measures intelligence, we would correlate it with other known intelligence scores, with school performance, or with various measures of problem solving. The LPC score has now been correlated with innumerable tests and measures, and none has yielded consistent relations. It is obvious from this lack of findings that the LPC score taps a personality attribute which is not measured by the usual psychological tests. However, considering the high predictive power of the score in such complex and socially relevant interactions as leadership, there can be little doubt that we are dealing with a very important aspect of personality.

LPC AND LEADER BEHAVIOR

While personality tests and questionnaires do not tell us much about the nature of LPC, member descriptions and observations of leaders do provide a more consistent picture. In general, the high LPC leader is seen as more considerate, more human relations-oriented, more participative in his management style, and more sensitive to the feelings of others. The low LPC leader tends to be seen as more directive, more structuring, more goal oriented, and more concerned with efficiency. By and large, however, the differences in the behaviors of high and low LPC leaders tend to be relatively small and subtle.

Situational favorableness

Since the LPC score correlates positively with leader performance in some situations but negatively in others, it seems reasonable to expect that the leader's personality must in some way interact with the favorableness of the situation, that is, with the degree to which the situation provides the leader with control and influence. This has now been demonstrated by a substantial number of studies (see Fiedler, 1972).

Let us take the two important leader behaviors, consideration and initiation of structure, as rated by observers, and compare leaders in situations in which they have relatively great and relatively little control. This gives us the results in Figure 6–1. These data come from a study of three-man teams of ROTC cadets which performed problem-solving and creative tasks under relatively stress-free and relatively stressful conditions (Fiedler, 1967). The former situation was made as relaxed and nonthreatening as possible, while, in the stressful situation, the men were in uniform, the situation was quite formal, and an army major, lieutenant colonel, or colonel whom the men had never seen before sat across the table from each group and took notes throughout the session.

As can be seen in Figure 6–1, the high LPC leaders were rated as low in relationship-concerned behavior and high in task-relevant behavior in the more favorable, low-stress condition. They were rated as high in relationship concern and low in task concern in the more stressful condition. In contrast, low LPC leaders were more concerned with the relationship and less concerned with the task in the low-stress condition, and more concerned with the task and less with the relationship in the more stressful, less favorable situation.

A study by Sample and Wilson (1965) shows that the same leaders dramatically change behavior as the situation changes. The groups in their experiment were conducting class projects involving a laboratory rat in a maze learning problem. At the same time, the students were rated by trained observers using Bales' system (1951). Each group had to plan, execute, and prepare a report of the study. These three phases of the experiment differed in degree of task structure. Running the rat through the maze was the most structured phase, writing the report was somewhat structured, and planning the experiment was a quite unstructured subtask.

Shirakashi (personal communication), who reanalyzed the Sample and Wilson data, showed that the low LPC leaders made more positive social-emotional responses in the running phase and relatively few in the planning phase, while the high LPC leaders made the most task-relevant statements in the running phase but relatively few in the

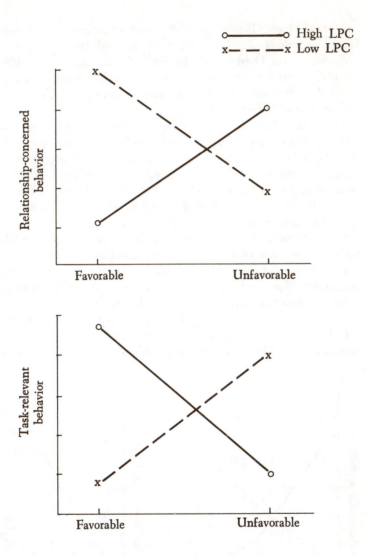

FIGURE 6–1.   Interaction Between Leader LPC and Situational Favorableness (Stress) in the ROTC Study. Source: Fiedler, F. E., *Leadership*,
p. 15, Morristown, N.J.: General Learning Press. © 1971 General Learning
Corporation.

planning phase (Figure 6–2). A number of other studies show very similar results (e.g., Ayer, 1968; Morris and Fiedler, 1964; Fiedler, Meuwese, and Oonk, 1961; Fiedler, O'Brien, and Ilgen, 1969). Of course, in cases where even the more favorable situations are stressful or anxiety arousing, the results do not always come out so neatly (e.g., Chemers and Skrzypek, 1972).

What are the implications of these findings? First of all, the results demonstrate that the leader's behavior is not consistent over situations. Leaders tend to behave in a human relations-centered manner in one situation but in a job-centered manner in another. *This means that we cannot define leadership style by leader behavior.* There are no generally considerate leaders, only leaders who are considerate in some situations and inconsiderate in others.

Second, these and similar findings once again show the overriding importance of the situation. Whether or not the way in which we have defined situational favorableness is the last word—and better methods will surely be developed—it seems clear that the situation must play an important part in affecting the leader's behavior.

This can also be seen in the way in which the leader affects the satisfaction of his group members. If the low LPC leader is more considerate in very favorable situations while the high LPC leader is more

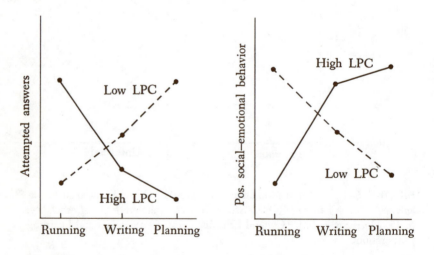

FIGURE 6–2.   Sample and Wilson (1965) Data Reanalyzed by Shirakashi (Personal Communication). Source: Fiedler, 1971b. Reproduced by permission of Rotterdam University Press.

considerate in unfavorable situations, this will be reflected in group member satisfaction. Not surprisingly, group members are more satisfied with low LPC leaders in favorable situations but more satisfied with high LPC leaders in less favorable situations (Fiedler, O'Brien, and Ilgen, 1969). Thus, if we wish to increase group member satisfaction, we should place the low LPC leaders in very favorable situations and high LPC leaders in less favorable situations.

It is important to note at this point that the Contingency Model and other theories of group effectiveness are here in basic agreement when they point out that considerate or employee-centered leaders tend to have effective groups. The Contingency Model also finds that low LPC leaders are effective as well as considerate in very favorable situations, and that high LPC leaders are considerate and effective in moderately favorable situations. We part company in the least favorable situations in which the low LPC leaders are again effective but the high LPC leaders are more considerate.

Is the Contingency Model really different from other theories? The answer is clearly yes. The Contingency Model *predicts* on the basis of an LPC score which can be obtained *prior* to assembling the groups. The other theories merely show that there is an association between behavior and performance. This implies that the combination of LPC and situational favorableness determines behavior and performance, while most other theories have only shown that there is an association between leader behavior and performance.

An interpretation of LPC

Now let us return to the earlier question of how to interpret the LPC score. The data on leader behaviors make it quite clear that neither high nor low LPC persons behave consistently in one way or another. As we saw from Figures 6–1, 6–2, and 6–3, in favorable situations high LPC persons tend to concentrate on the task while low LPC persons concern themselves with developing good relations. Moreover, high LPC persons also tend to describe themselves as more concerned with the task while low LPC persons describe themselves as more concerned with good interpersonal relations (see Fiedler, 1972).

This makes sense if we assume that a person generally thinks of how he behaves when he is in control of the situation, that is, when he is accepted and respected as a leader, when he knows how to handle the task, and when he has some power to obtain member

FIGURE 6–3.   Effective Leadership and Considerate Leader Behaviors in Situations of Different Favorableness.

Relationship Motivation	Situational Favorableness		
	Very favorable	Moderately favorable	Unfavorable
Relationship-motivated (High LPC)	Ineffective	Effective	Ineffective
	Inconsiderate	Considerate	Considerate
Task-motivated (Low LPC)	Effective	Ineffective	Effective
	Considerate	Inconsiderate	Inconsiderate

compliance. After all, few people, when they are asked how they normally behave as leaders, will imagine themselves to be disliked and rejected, unable to figure out how to do the job, and without much power. In fact, the way they describe themselves is also the way they tend to behave in the favorable situation. Unfortunately, however, most of one's life as a leader is spent in situations which are not quite so favorable. Typically, we are not quite sure how to get the job accomplished, and frequently we are not sure of the backing our group members are willing to give us. Hence, we are often observed as we behave in situations which are not truly favorable.

Consider, for example, the many observational studies of laboratory groups. Here the leaders as a rule have relatively little power, first of all because they are dealing with ad hoc groups, and second because the typical laboratory group task is of the problem-solving variety or requires some type of creative performance, rather than highly structured assembly tasks where every member knows exactly how to do his job.

We have interpreted the LPC score as an index of the hierarchy of goals and needs by which each person orders his priorities and, therefore, his behavior. To repeat, when the situation is relatively stressful and provides the leader with inadequate power and influence, he will seek to accomplish those goals which to him are most important. For the high LPC person, these are relations with others, the needs for affection, approval, and status. For the low LPC person, these needs involve task accomplishment.

When the situation is very favorable, when the leader's control and influence are sufficient to assure the attainment of his goals, he will seek to obtain his secondary goals, the "luxuries" of his life. The high LPC leader, who in the very favorable situation is assured of his group's acceptance, will now seek status and esteem from others (e.g., his superiors). The low LPC leader in the highly favorable situation also is assured of his major goal, task accomplishment. He knows how to do the job since it is highly structured, and he has the wherewithal to do it—his group's support and the power to obtain compliance. He can therefore relax and be pleasant about it. Business before pleasure, but business with pleasure where possible!

Labeling the individual as high or low LPC is, of course, somewhat arbitrary. From the standpoint of personality theory, it would seem more appropriate to view the individual's behavior under stress as the more accurate reflection of his "basic" personality. For this reason, we have called the high LPC persons relationship-motivated and the low LPC persons task-motivated.

SUMMARY

What do the findings which we have presented in this chapter tell us? First, there is no one-to-one relation between leadership behavior and the leader's personality—hence, leader behavior is not leadership style. Rather, the leader's behavior changes in a predictable direction, depending upon the leader's personality and the degree to which the situation gives him influence and control. Hence, teaching a leader to behave in a certain way may be a very inefficient method for making him perform better since the behavior is only the surface manifestation of his personality as it interacts with situational factors.

Second, the key personality variable in the Contingency Model, the Least Preferred Coworker score, is an index of a motivational hierarchy. Individuals appear to pursue their more basic goals in unfavorable situations in which they are uncertain and threatened; they pursue their secondary goals in favorable situations in which they feel that their primary or basic goals are secure. The high LPC persons seek as their basic goal to be related to others but as their secondary goal esteem and status. The low LPC persons seek as their basic goal the accomplishment of the task, but as their secondary goal the maintenance of a good work relationship with group members.

REFERENCES

Ayer, J. G. "Effects of success and failure of interpersonal and task performance upon leader perception and behavior." Unpublished master's thesis, University of Illinois, Urbana, 1968.

Bales, R. F. *Interaction Process Analysis.* Harvard University Press, 1951.

Campbell, J. P., M. D. Dunnette, E. E. Lawler, III, and K. E. Weick. *Managerial Behavior, Performance, and Effectiveness.* McGraw-Hill, 1970.

Chemers, M. M., and G. J. Skrzypek. "An experimental test of the Contingency Model of leadership effectiveness." *Journal of Personality and Social Psychology* 24 (1972): 172–77.

Coch, L., and J. R. P. French, Jr. "Overcoming resistance to change." *Human Relations* 1 (1948): 512–32.

Fiedler, F. E. *A Theory of Leadership Effectiveness.* McGraw-Hill, 1967.

Fiedler, F. E. *Leadership.* General Learning Press, 1971a.

Fiedler, F. E. *The Perceived Role of the Military.* Rotterdam University Press, 1971b, p. 196.

Fiedler, F. E. "Personality, motivational systems, and behavior of high and low LPC persons." *Human Relations* 25 (1972): 391–412.

Fiedler, F. E., W. A. T. Meuwese, and S. Oonk. "Performance of laboratory tasks requiring group creativity." *Acta Psychologica* 18 (1961): 100–119.

Fiedler, F. E., G. E. O'Brien, and D. R. Ilgen. "The effect of leadership style upon the performance and adjustment of volunteer teams operating in a stressful environment." *Human Relations* 22 (1969): 503–14.

Korman, A. "The prediction of managerial performance: A review." *Personnel Psychology* 21 (1968): 259–322.

Likert, R. *New Patterns of Management.* McGraw-Hill, 1961.

Morris, C. G., and F. E. Fiedler. "Application of a new system of interaction analysis to the relationship between leader attitudes and behavior in problem-solving groups." Group Effectiveness Research Laboratory, University of Illinois, Urbana, 1964.

Morse, N. C., and E. Reimer. "The experimental change of a major organizational variable." *Journal of Abnormal and Social Psychology* 52 (1956): 120–29.

Nealey, S. M., and M. R. Blood. "Leadership performance of nursing supervisors at two organizational levels." *Journal of Applied Psychology* 52 (1968): 414–21.

Robinson, J. P., and P. R. Shaver. *Measures of Social Psychological Attitudes.* Institute for Social Research, University of Michigan, 1969.

Sample, J. A., and T. R. Wilson. "Leader behavior, group productivity, and rating of least preferred co-worker." *Journal of Personality and Social Psychology* 13 (1965): 266–70.

Stogdill, R. M., and A. E. Coons. "Leader behavior: Its description and measurement." Research Monograph No. 88. Ohio State University, 1957.

Vroom, V. H. *Some Personality Determinants of the Effects of Participation.* Prentice-Hall, 1960.

The Leader in Complex Organizations

7

The interaction approach which we have taken throughout the previous chapters tells us that neither the personality of the leader nor the characteristics of his particular work group, by themselves, explain the group's performance. The question which we wish to explore in this chapter deals with the part which the larger organization plays in the leadership process.

We have so far based our arguments and conclusions largely upon empirical evidence, but we will now combine hard data with a dash of speculation and conjecture. Our aim is not to write the final chapter on organizational leadership or even to provide an exhaustive review of the area. Rather, we hope to point out directions and possibilities in the application of the contingency theory of leadership to complex organizational problems.

A considerable number of eminent theorists and researchers have held that certain attributes of the leader, or certain characteristics of the organization, are related to performance. While this is unquestionably true, the problem is that the degree to which each of these organizational or personality variables contribute to organizational performance tends to be either small and inconsistent or not generalizable from one organization to another. A recent review identified four major approaches to organizational performance:

1) Traditional structuralist theories;
2) Modern structuralist theories;
3) Personalistic theories;
4) Integrative or interaction theories.

108

Let us briefly examine the assumptions and implications of each of these approaches.

Structural approaches to organization, both traditional and modern, are based on the premise that a global theory of organizations can be constructed. "Since all men are seen as basically similar by the structural theories, 'one best way' to organize and administer all men can be generated. Traditional and modern structural theorists differ strongly in their analysis of the specific characteristics of men and the 'one best way' to manage, but they hold in common the view that there is, indeed, 'one best way'" (Lichtman and Hunt, 1971).

The traditional structuralist or classical organization theories are typified by the scientific management approach of Frederick Taylor (1911). They maintain that man is basically lazy, untrustworthy, and motivated by material gain. The organizational model which naturally results from this view is the bureaucracy with its emphasis on efficiency maximization through rules, spans of control, and extrinsic incentives.

Following the same basic logic, the modern structuralists begin from a completely different premise. All men are seen as interested in self-actualization or the realization of their full potential. Characterized by the work of such theorists as Argyris (1964) and McGregor (1967), the modern structuralists propose organizations which are loose and open, allowing employees to reach self-actualization through participative decision-making, face-to-face work groups, and mutual confidence between superior and subordinate. The basic premise underlying this position is that the organization has a responsibility to society and to its employees and that this responsibility has for too long been neglected.

The personalistic theories are directly opposed to the structural and "one best way" approaches. Theories in this category stress individual cognitive attributes and individual differences in the perception of, and reaction to, the organization (e.g., Maslow, 1965). They stress that people's needs, motives, and values determine how they react to their organizational environment. The personalistic theorists make some relevant points in their emphasis on the influence of informal work groups, employer's values and expectancies, and individual differences in role perception and fulfillment. On the other hand, in their preoccupation with the individual they tend to say very little about the formal organization itself.

The integrative approach to organization is best expressed by Scott (1967) in his discussion of modern organization theory. "Human behavior in organizational settings can be understood in terms of three elements (a) the stated design of functions, that is, the requirements of the organization; (b) the characteristics of people who populate the organization, that is, the attributes they bring with them into the organization, including those derived from other social affiliations; (c) the relations between the organization's defined properties and the characteristics of people who 'populate it'" (Lichtman and Hunt, 1971, p. 271). The integrative approach attempts to bring together elements of both the structuralistic and personalistic views. It tries to avoid the concept of the "one best way" to organize.

An interaction theory of leadership, like the Contingency Model, falls into the integrative category of organizational theories. It emphasizes the importance of the formal organization in determining the nature of the leadership situation. At the same time, it stresses the way in which the individual personality and motivational patterns interact with situational features to determine leader and managerial effectiveness, and, of course, organizational effectiveness.

ORGANIZATIONAL CLIMATE

One of the most important concepts in current organization theory is the "organizational climate," which we have described in a previous chapter. There are now a considerable number of operational measures which identify the type of climate which characterizes an organization. However, there is very little empirical evidence from field studies that one type of climate is necessarily more conducive to effective organizational performance than another. While such a relationship is claimed on the basis of several laboratory studies (e.g., Litwin and Stringer, 1966), it seems premature to generalize from these to the behavior of real-life organizations. Whether or not certain organizational climates produce, or are associated with, more effective performance, it seems likely that organizational climate will interact with the leader's task- or relationship-motivation in affecting organizational performance.

This hypothesis, extending the Contingency Model, was tested by Csoka (1972) in a recent study of 52 army companies and their mess halls. The specific focus of the study was the influence of the parent organization (the company) on the performance of the subordinate unit, here the mess hall. The performance criterion consisted of ratings by the company commander as well as the brigade food service officer who oversees the food service of about nine company

mess halls in his brigade. These two ratings had a high (.85) correlation with each other, and they also correlated (.45) with the opinions
of randomly selected soldiers from each of the companies.

Csoka used as his basis for measuring organizational climate the
Burns and Stalker (1961) classification of *mechanistic* versus *organic*
climates. The mechanistic climate stresses vertical authority relations,
detailed job instructions, rules and regulations, etc. The organic climate
is typified by lateral as well as upward and downward communication,
by a rather fluid organizational structure which changes as the tasks
change, and by rules and guidelines which are easily modified.

In terms of the Contingency Model, the mechanistic environment would, of course, present a relatively favorable leadership situation since the task as well as the lines of authority are highly structured
and the leader knows exactly where he stands. In contrast, the organic
climate is by definition unstructured and considerably less stable.

Csoka derived organizational climate measures from descriptions of the organization which he obtained from all key personnel of
the company (company commander, executive officer, cadre) as well
as from the mess steward and his cooks. He found that the mess halls
assigned to octant v were described as having organic climates, while
the organizations in all other octants fell into the mechanistic category.
(Since the study dealt with military units, the preponderance of mechanistic organizational climates is not too surprising.) As Csoka predicted, the relationship-motivated, high LPC leaders performed best in
the units described as having an organic climate while the task-
motivated leaders performed best in units described as having a
mechanistic climate. The correlations between leader LPC and mess
hall performance were negative for the units with mechanistic climates
and positive for those with organic ones (-0.51 and $+0.57$, $n = 17$).

This study is important for two reasons. First of all, it provides
a bridge between the Contingency Model and a large area of organization theory which has been relatively unconcerned with an interactional
approach to leadership. Second, it shows how the larger organization
affects the operation of its subunits.

PARTICIPATIVE MANAGEMENT

A second study which relates leadership theory to organizational research was recently conducted by Blades and Fiedler (1973).
These data too came from the mess hall study, but the particular focus

of this investigation was the effect of group member participation on group performance. As we have pointed out previously, there have been a number of studies which show a slight advantage of participative types of management over nonparticipative approaches to decision-making. While there has been considerable interest in this problem, the empirical research testing the efficacy of participative management has been surprisingly sparse (Campbell et al., 1970, p. 422).

The problem is of interest for a number of reasons. First of all, the question arises whether all leaders are equally likely to use participative decision-making, and we would suspect that this is not so. It would seem reasonable to expect that relationship-motivated leaders, who are concerned about the opinions and attitudes of their members, would be more likely to consult them in planning and policy making, but an even more important question is the following. Let us suppose that an individual in the leadership position is fully committed to group decision-making. Would the quality of the decisions, and hence the effectiveness of the organization, then not depend upon the intellectual abilities of the group members? If this is the case, we would expect good decisions and good performance from intelligent groups but poor decisions and hence poor performance from relatively dull groups. The average performance of groups with participative leadership (that is, high LPC leaders) should then be about as high as the average performance of groups which do not participate in the decision-making process, and there should be a positive correlation between group member intelligence and group performance for groups which participate in decision-making. The corresponding correlation should be essentially zero for groups in which the leader does not involve his groups in the decision-making processes.

Blades and Fiedler conducted three different studies, one using Csoka's mess hall data, one on 27 squads of a combat engineer battalion, and one on teen-age teams conducting public health work. In each of these studies, the group members' intelligence correlated with performance only in groups of high LPC leaders, not in groups of low LPC leaders. And just as expected, group members under high LPC leaders indicated on questionnaires that they had been involved in the planning and participation stage while members of low LPC leaders did not. The average performances of groups with participative and nonparticipative leadership were not basically different.

We definitely require much more research before we can say how generalizable these findings might be. It is obvious, however, that the simple prescription of "participative management for better performance" cannot be taken without serious qualifications. It should be used only for relationship-motivated leaders and only in groups in which the participants in the decision-making processes are of comparatively high intelligence or especially knowledgeable.

CHANGES IN MANAGERIAL POSITION

Changes in the leadership situation resulting from promotion, leadership succession, and job rotation, as well as from turnover in subordinate personnel and from changes in assignment, are one major effect of the organization on its leaders. The important consequences of these changes depend upon the answers to two crucial questions. As phrased in terms of the Contingency Model, they are:

1) How does the favorableness of the new situation differ from that of the old?
2) How does the leader's personality and motivational system match the demands of the new situation?

Promotion

An increase in rank typically involves a promotion to a higher level in the organization. This may mean that the manager now supervises a larger organization, with more employees, or that he has been assigned to a staff position, or that his new job involves the supervision of fewer employees, as with the plant manager who moves up to be assistant to the vice-president, or the company legal counsel who becomes company manager.

In general, as Katz and Kahn (1966) have pointed out, managers at the lower organizational levels typically deal with more highly structured tasks. The first-level supervisor or foreman is likely to supervise day-to-day production, where the number of policy decisions and problems requiring new and creative solutions is typically small. At the same time, he has a fairly high degree of authority. While there has been considerable discussion of the powerlessness of the first-level supervisor or foreman, his authority to assign men to jobs, his prerogatives to recommend certain disciplinary measures, and his legitimate power over certain aspects of the job are rarely challenged.

To be sure, this is a far cry from the almost unlimited power the foreman used to have in the not so good old days around the turn of the century when he was the unchallenged autocrat of the shop floor. However, even within the strict limitations on his decision-making powers which a union contract might spell out, his position power is still considerable.

At the middle or upper levels of management, the tasks tend to be notably less structured. Complex decisions may be called for, and the jobs at these levels often involve considerable coordination of human and technical resources. The middle- or upper-level managerial job frequently tends to be of moderate situational favorableness. In the typical case of promotion to a middle-management position, the individual frequently moves from a very favorable situation into one which is only moderately favorable for the leader. Likewise, the junior executive who has been the assistant to a plant manager or a vice-president may be promoted to a line job; he may move from a position of intermediate favorableness to one in which the situation is highly favorable.

Obviously, not all first-level management positions are highly favorable, nor are all middle-management positions necessarily of moderate favorableness. A foreman who is not accepted by his group will have a moderately favorable position even though his position power is high and his task is structured. An accepted middle manager with a structured line job will have a favorable situation. Our examples only illustrate the possible change in favorableness as the individual is promoted from one level of the organization to another; his success will depend upon the degree to which his motivational system matches the demands of the new situation.

To give two specific examples, we conducted a study of 32 farm supply companies (Godfrey et al., 1959), each of which was supervised by a board of directors with implementation of board policy in the hands of a general manager. The criterion of performance consisted of the percent net income of total sales and percent and operating costs of total sales volume. In harmonious companies, where the manager was accepted by his staff as well as by the board, task-motivated general managers performed better than did relationship-motivated managers. However, relationship-motivated board presidents had better performing companies than did task-motivated board presidents.

A similar finding comes from a study by Nealey and Blood (1968) of a psychiatric nursing organization. These authors found that the task-motivated first-level supervisors, the head nurses, were rated as performing better than relationship-motivated head nurses, while their superiors, the unit supervisors, performed better when relationship-motivated. Note that in both of these organizations the task of the second-level managers was considerably less structured than was the task of managers at the first level of the organization.

Where the jobs are similar at the first and second levels, we do not find such a reversal. Thus, the jobs of both the first-level and second-level foremen in an open-hearth steel plant are highly structured. As expected, we found that the accepted senior *and* junior melters who were task-motivated performed better than did those who were relationship-motivated. Performance of the first-level manager should predict the performance after promotion to senior melter since the situations are similar in favorableness. However, promotion of a head nurse to unit supervisor, or promotion of a general manager to president of the board of directors in a farm supply company, would present a very different leadership situation and hence a considerably higher chance that the individual would become less effective in his new job.

While the studies cited here do not provide an extensive test of contingency theory applications for promotion, some tentative conclusions are justified. Organizational theorists generally agree that job demands differ strongly as a function of organizational level. These job demands can meaningfully be classified in terms of situational favorableness. It follows, then, that promotion will result in maximum organizational effectiveness if the match between the leader's orientation and the situational demands is taken into account.

Leadership rotation and succession

Whenever a senior employee has retired or been discharged, promoted, or transferred, someone must be found to fill his old job. Considering the frequency with which leadership successions occur, it is amazing that so little research has been published on this topic. A brief review by Gibb (1969) is available in the *Handbook of Social Psychology,* and Champion (unpublished, 1971) recently completed a more extensive survey of the literature. The main conclusions to be drawn from available research are that leadership succession creates turbulence and instability in the organizational structure, and the better the organization prepares itself for these shifts in leadership the less instability will result. In general, the literature provides a rather glum and pessimistic picture which emphasizes the negative aspects of this problem.

Another aspect of managerial change is job rotation, which will be discussed in the next chapter. Rotation policies figure widely in managerial training and development programs (Wickstrom [1964]) found rotation used as a recognized management development technique in 72 percent of the companies he studied), but rarely is an effort made to provide this type of experience in a well-planned and systematic fashion.

It is important to note at this point that the difference between rotation and succession is rather minor. Rotation typically implies a deliberate shift of managers from one position on an organizational level to another position on the same organizational level, and usually for the purpose of cross-training managers so that they will have a broader perspective on organizational problems. Succession typically implies promotion to a higher level, or transfer to another job at the same level for the purpose of improving organizational performance or staffing a job, rather than for the purpose of providing more experience or training to the manager who is being moved.

Whether the change is due to rotation or succession, we can be quite certain that the personality and leadership style of the predecessor will play a large part in the welcome accorded to his successor. In organizations in which any change will be seen as an improvement, the new leader will usually gain ready acceptance. In groups which have just lost their hero, especially as a result of his conflict with the organization, the new leader may find himself in a very unpleasant and difficult situation which is not at all of his making. Whether or not the change will result in improved performance should, however, depend upon the way in which the leader's motivational system matches the new situation in which he finds himself. That the outcome need not be detrimental to performance is shown by an extremely interesting and daring field experiment on the effect of rotating well liked and disliked managers.

Rosen (1969), working with the management of a furniture manufacturing plant, obtained the sociometric choices of employees for their foremen. He then arranged to have the foremen switched from department to department so that the foremen who were most liked by their subordinates were moved to departments which had disliked their former foremen and vice versa. The result of this rotation turned out to be a sudden spurt of productivity in all departments which remained for some time and then gradually declined. Rosen's study showed that the disruption which did occur was beneficial rather than detrimental to performance. It at least got people out of their ruts.

Above all, the policy of rotating management personnel provides the company with an opportunity to observe the manager in a wide variety of situations, and permits the further selection of those who somehow perform well in all of the jobs to which they have been assigned. It also enables the manager to determine those conditions in which he feels most comfortable and is most effective. Finally, it enables the manager to meet and work with a number of others with whom he will have contact throughout his career.

While the managerial job rotation policies are very attractive in principle, only rarely is someone permitted the privilege of failing on a job. This is, however, quite likely to happen if the job to which he is assigned does not happen to match his motivational system. Thus, a relationship-motivated manager might be assigned to a highly favorable or highly unfavorable situation and perform poorly, ending up as someone who "bombed out." This means that the organization is likely to lose a substantial number of otherwise excellent managers because it is assumed that everyone who moves ahead must be outstanding on each and every job to which he is assigned.

This is explicitly the policy of the armed services, and while it may have served well once, when almost every officer's assignment was a line job in charge of a unit, it is probably detrimental to the development of an outstanding officer corps at a time when many jobs are unstructured. We expect supermen, but we may only get those who are able to get by, especially when the system does not permit, in practice, anything but ratings of "outstanding" and "superior"; a rating of "good" or "average" means total failure.

A similar conclusion was reached by Major Phillip W. Mock (1972) who reviewed a series of internal U.S. Army studies of officer career development. Mock observed that the current career system in the Army requires each officer to gain a wide variety of job experience through a pattern of short-term, highly diversified assignments which often require him to work in an area drastically removed from his own specialty. He concluded that this pattern of diversified assignments worked to the detriment of a highly professional officer corps and resulted in considerable levels of dissatisfaction among young officers. Referring to the notion that one man can succeed in all positions and be, in effect, the perfect soldier, Mock chose to title his article "Delusions of Grandeur."

CONCLUSION AND IMPLICATIONS

We have tried to point out to the reader some ways in which the contingency theory is relevant to the problems of modern organizations. The material presented in this chapter is not meant as a comprehensive analysis of organizational psychology, but only to show how certain aspects of organizational functioning (i.e, leadership succession, organizational structure, and problem demands) can influence situational favorableness for a leader. No leadership theory can possibly explain all the problems of organization. On the other hand, a valid and comprehensive leadership theory can offer many insights into managerial effectiveness. Organizations are made up of people, and many of these people are leaders. The contingency theory can help us to explain, predict, and influence their performance.

REFERENCES

Argyris, C. *Integrating the Individual and the Organization*. Wiley, 1964.

Blades, J. W., and F. E. Fiedler. "The influence of group member intelligence on group performance: A Contingency Model study." Paper presented at the Western Psychological Association Meetings, April 11–14, 1973.

Burns, T., and G. M. Stalker. *The Management of Innovation*. Quadrangle, 1961.

Campbell, J. P., M. D. Dunnette, E. E. Lawler, III, and K. E. Weick. *Managerial Behavior, Performance, and Effectiveness*. McGraw-Hill, 1970.

Champion, J. "Managerial succession in complex organizations." University of Washington (mimeograph), 1971.

Csoka, L. S. "A validation of the Contingency Model approach to leadership experience and training." Technical Report No. 72–32. Organizational Research Group, University of Washington, 1972.

Gibb, C. A. "Leadership." In *The Handbook of Social Psychology*, G. Lindzey and E. Aronson, eds., pp. 205–82. Addison-Wesley, 1969.

Godfrey, E. P., F. E. Fiedler, and D. M. Hall. *Boards, Managers, and Company Success*. Interstate Press, 1959.

Katz, D., and R. L. Kahn. *The Social Psychology of Organizations*. Wiley, 1966.

Lichtman, C. M., and R. G. Hunt. "Personality and organization theory: A review of some conceptual literature." *Psychological Bulletin* 76 (1971): 271–94.

Litwin, C. H., and R. Stringer. "The influence of organization climate on human motivation." Paper presented at a conference on Organizational Climate, Foundation for Research on Human Behavior, Ann Arbor, Mich., March 1966.

McGregor, D. *The Professional Manager*. McGraw-Hill, 1967.

Maslow, A. H. *Eupsychian Management*. Irwin, 1965.

Mock, P. W. "Delusions of grandeur." *Military Review* 52 (1972): 50–65.

Nealey, S. M., and M. R. Blood. "Leadership performance of nursing supervisors at two organizational levels." *Journal of Applied Psychology* 52 (1968): 414–21.

Rosen, N. A. *Leadership Change and Work-Group Dynamics: An Experiment*. Cornell University Press, 1969.

Scott, W. G. *Organization Theory: A Behavioral Analysis for Management*. Irwin, 1967.

Taylor, F. W. *The Principles of Scientific Management*. Harper & Row, 1911.

Wickstrom, W. S. "Developing managerial competence: Changing concepts—emerging practices." National Industrial Conference Board Studies in Personnel Policy, No. 189, 1964.

Leadership Training and Experience

8

How to make the leader and the organization more effective is the ultimate question of any book on leadership. Organizations spend literally billions of dollars each year on management development and supervisory training. The training may focus on increasing production or employee satisfaction, on improving interpersonal relations, or on broadening the individual's horizons in the hope that his productivity or effectiveness will ultimately be increased.

We occasionally hear that the goals of training are self-actualization of the manager or improved employee relations, but though this may be a popular belief in some academic circles, it is not shared by most members of the business community. England (1967) asked 1972 managers throughout the country to indicate which of eight organizational goals are most important, and which indicate greatest success. Increasing organizational efficiency and high productivity received 60 percent of the votes, while employee and social welfare received only 4 and 2 percent respectively. This is not unreasonable. Business organizations exist by making a profit, not by performing philanthropic deeds, and this is likely to remain true even in an era of heightened social consciousness. For this reason, we shall focus on organizational performance as the goal of training.

HOW SUCCESSFUL IS LEADERSHIP TRAINING?

Considering the prodigious amounts of money and effort which

120

have been devoted to leadership training, it is essential that we take a hard and critical look at the benefits an organization may reasonably expect from such an undertaking. If leadership training is supposed to increase the effectiveness or productivity of an organization, what evidence do we have that it fulfills this purpose?

Unfortunately, provisions for objectively evaluating leadership training programs are the exception rather than the rule. Typically, when asked whether or not he knows if a program is effective, the training director will respond, "Of course it's effective. If it weren't, why would we be doing it?" Such faith may be heart-warming, but it is misplaced.

The state of the art: A brief critique

The actual research in the area of leadership and management training is not much more illuminating. A thorough review of training research (Campbell et al, 1970) cites 73 reported studies, 52 of which used "internal" evaluation criteria, questionnaires, interviews, or tests, to see if the trainee had learned anything. Not surprisingly, these results tended to be positive.

The typical trainee might receive, at great expense to his company, a full week of lectures, demonstrations, and films exhorting him to adopt a more considerate, interpersonally oriented style with his subordinates. He is then presented with a questionnaire designed to assess any changes in his attitudes. He should know enough by that time to check the most considerate and interpersonally oriented responses. In the rare cases in which behavior changes are assessed, they may in fact show a greater awareness of interpersonal relations and may slightly increase the supervisor's acceptance by his subordinates, though this is not invariably true. In a study of 126 post office managers, the amount of managerial training and various subordinate job satisfaction measures showed a median correlation of only .08 (Fiedler, Nealey, and Wood, 1968).

If, however, the ultimate goal of leadership training is an increase in the manager's ability to achieve organizational goals, then we cannot be satisfied with less than adequate performance criteria. Campbell et al., who make this point quite clearly, say:

". . . that the present empirical literature on the relationship of training content to management performance tells us very little about what kind of knowledge and skills contribute to managerial effectiveness. In order for this to happen, it *must* be demonstrated that 'what is learned' in a training program contributes to making the individual a better manager. For example, to be able to say that a positive attitude toward the human relations aspect of work contributes to managerial effectiveness, a change in such an attitude must be reflected by a change in performance" (p. 325).

The research based on such external criteria as productivity, grievance rates, labor turnover, and absenteeism does not arouse great confidence. Generally speaking, we can test for training effects only by correlation analysis, which shows whether a greater amount of training leads to correspondingly better performance, or by comparing the performances of trained managers with those of a comparable group of managers who did not receive training. Of the 21 studies in the Campbell review which yielded positive training effects on external criteria, only 13 had any kind of controls, that is, only 13 compared the trained and the untrained managers in some way.

In fact, most studies have failed to show that more leadership training results in better leadership performance, or that trained leaders perform better than untrained leaders, even though studies with negative or indefinite results rarely get published. It must be remembered, of course, that we are here talking about training in supervision, not the technical training a prospective manager must have before he can even be considered for an executive position: A man must first be a surgeon before he can head a surgical team; he must be a pilot before he can become the captain of an airliner. But even given these qualifications, the empirical evidence in support of the benefits of leadership training is far from rosy.

One of the most widely cited studies on the effects of supervisory training was carried out at the International Harvester Company by Fleishman, Harris, and Burtt (1955). These authors trained supervisors to behave in a more considerate and structuring manner. The training did not result in any consistent effects even on internal criteria. When such external criteria as absenteeism, accidents, grievances, turnover, and superior ratings were obtained, training seemed to have had positive effects in some departments, such as service, and negative effects in others, such as production. Also, the ratings by superiors often tended to be negatively related to such indices as absenteeism.

Another method of leadership training which has become popular within the last twenty years is the so-called T-group, laboratory method, or sensitivity training. Most of these approaches follow the same general format. A group of individuals is assembled, usually at an isolated residential training center or resort for a one-week program. In the typical T-group program, the trainer gives a minimum of instructions to the participants when they meet. As discussions develop about the purposes of the group, and the way in which various goals of the group can be met, the group members, under guidance of the training staff, analyze each other's and their own behaviors and reactions to the developing relationships. Without expert leadership these sessions may become quite stressful for the participants, and for some they have, in fact, resulted in adverse psychological reactions making it advisable to have the services of a well trained psychiatrist or clinical psychologist available. On the other hand, for many participants, the T-group or sensitivity group program represents a very interesting and personally involving experience which may provide the individual with important insights into his own behavior and into his reactions to the behaviors of others.

While there has been considerable research on the effect of T-group and sensitivity training on behavior (e.g., Schein, 1965; Bunker, 1967), practically all the findings relate to changes in behavior rather than in leadership performance. There is some evidence that many participants increase in interpersonal competence and that some individuals become more sensitive to the needs of others as a consequence of the T-group or laboratory experience. Here again, however, extensive reviews of the literature have not revealed any evidence that these types of training experience contribute to organizational performance of managers (Odiorne, 1964; House, 1967; Dunnette and Campbell, 1968).

There is also a widely held belief that the effective leadership training program must make the leader more "flexible" so that he can adapt himself to the changing demands of the situation. By enabling the leader to become more sensitive to others it should also increase his motivation to perform well. This is another attractive theory which has failed to live up to its billing. Since it is reasonable to assume that "flexibility" is present to a greater extent in some people than in others, it follows then that the flexible people should perform consistently well regardless of the task while the inflexible people might be good on one task but poor on another. If this were so we would expect at least moderately high performance correlations across tasks for groups which have the same leader. As we have pointed out in a previous chapter, this is clearly not the case. Moreover, there is at this time no evidence that leaders scoring high on flexibility scales perform better than leaders who score low on scales of this type.

As we have been shown by the Contingency Model, different types of leaders tend to perform best in different situations. It would follow, therefore, that the same type of leader will not be successful in all situations. It further follows that the same type of leadership training is not likely to be effective for everyone. Yet most leadership training is implicitly geared to produce an ideal leader. Most human relations training programs assume that the best leader is one who is considerate and sensitive to the needs of his employees. The orthodox supervisory programs assume that the best leader is someone who clearly plans and decisively executes his plan by structuring and delegating tasks.

Some training programs have been very explicit in how the ideal leader should behave. One of the most widely known is the "Managerial Grid" developed by Blake and Mouton (1964). This training approach is based on the theory that the ideal leader is highly concerned with the task as well as with interpersonal relations. The program is designed to show managers where, on each of two nine-point scales measuring these two important behaviors, they fit, and how they can learn to become a "9.9 leader" (i.e., able to achieve maximum concern both for the person and for task accomplishment). This very attractive theory has found many enthusiastic supporters, but the evidence which Blake and his associates have produced has not been convincing.

Comparisons of trained and untrained leaders

Because it is extremely important to appreciate the fact that even the most intensive type of training does not increase leadership performance on the average, we shall here briefly summarize two well-controlled experiments and two correlational field studies.

One of the studies (Fiedler, 1966) compared the performance of 48 petty officers and 48 recruit leaders (see Chapter 2). Three-man groups, matched for intelligence and leadership style, performed four tasks, consisting of (A) composing a recruiting letter urging young men to join the Belgian navy, (B) routing a ship through 10 ports, (C) routing a ship through 12 ports, and (D) nonverbally demonstrating to the group members how to disassemble and reassemble an automatic pistol.

Petty officers in the Belgian naval forces typically attend a two-year petty-officer school which provides technical and leadership training. The graduate of this school then signs up for a twenty-year enlistment period. In other words, the Belgian petty officer is a well-trained and dedicated career man. In our study, the petty officers also scored higher on motivation and morale items than did the recruits.

We compared the performances of the petty officers, who, incidentally, had an average of ten years of leadership experience, with the performances of the recruits, who had been in the naval service less than six weeks. As Figure 8–1 shows, the differences between the

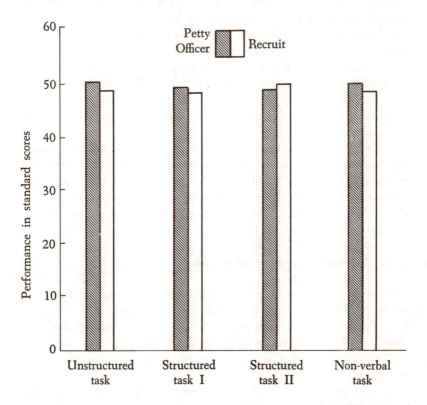

FIGURE 8–1.   Comparison of Belgian Navy Groups Led by Petty Officers and Recruits in Four Different Tasks. Source: Fiedler, 1971. Reprinted by permission.

petty officers and the recruit leaders were negligible. On not one of the four tasks did the petty officers perform significantly or substantially better than the recruit leaders.

A validation study (Fiedler and Chemers, 1968) was subsequently conducted in the context of a leadership workshop for officers of Canadian military academies. The officers in this study were captains and majors with five to seventeen years of military experience. All of them had attended a four-year military academy, and all officers were superior in measured intelligence to a sample of enlisted men. The enlisted men in this study were between 18 and 23 years old, and had just completed their eight weeks of basic training.

To reduce possible anxiety or awkwardness in working with officers, the enlisted men were told that they would work with "civilian instructors." Eight groups were headed by officers and seven by enlisted men. The tasks consisted of (A) writing a fable for school children to illustrate why Canada required a standing army, (B) routing a ship convoy, and (C) drawing bar graphs from score distributions. Despite the extensive leadership training and experience, as well as the intellectual superiority, of the officers, the teams led by them again performed no better than did the teams led by the inexperienced and untrained enlisted men.

To check whether these results were not simply due to the experimental nature of the tasks, we conducted two field studies in ongoing organizations. The first of these involved 171 post office managers and supervisors from 23 different post offices (Fiedler et al., 1968). We obtained data on the manager's previous training and then correlated the amount of training with the performance ratings he received from two to four of his superiors. These correlations between rated effectiveness and hours of technical and regional training outside the post office turned out to be essentially zero or slightly negative (0.04, −0.01, and −0.12, respectively). Correlating the average training received by all top managers of 12 post offices and various objective post office performance indices also yielded nonsignificant findings. In fact, 12 of 15 correlations were somewhat negative. Clearly, therefore, the amount of training did not improve a man's managerial performance.

A study of 15 police patrol sergeants gave identical results. Correlations between amount of supervisory training received and rated performance were around zero. Here too, supervisory training did not contribute to leadership performance.

LEADERSHIP EXPERIENCE

Let us now briefly look at leadership or managerial experience —basically on-the-job training—and its effect on performance. We assume that a person will learn something from having held a managerial position for several years. Moreover, a manager does get a great deal of informal training by his fellow supervisors as well as his superiors in the form of guidance and advice.

A paper by Fiedler (1970) reanalyzed data obtained from several studies by our group as well as by others. These included not only the experiments with Belgian and Canadian military personnel, but also studies of managers of consumer cooperatives, post office managers, directors of chemical research and development teams, managers of meat and grocery markets in a large food store chain, and foremen in craft shops and a heavy machinery plant. In all, the paper covered findings from 13 different groups encompassing 385 managers and leaders. In each case, the number of years of leadership experience was correlated with rated or objectively scored leadership performance. The median correlation for all 13 groups was −0.12 (Table 8–1).

A number of other studies not included in this analysis have given essentially similar results. These include studies of, for example, the police sergeants mentioned earlier, a group of school administrators (McNamara, 1968), and leaders of various types of military units. Nor are these data out of the ordinary. Younger leaders often perform better than older, more experienced ones. (Charles Percy, Toscanini, Joan of Arc, and the English Prime Minister William Pitt are good examples.)

A REINTERPRETATION OF LEADERSHIP TRAINING AND EXPERIENCE

How do we explain these findings? Is all leadership experience and training worthless? Are leaders really born rather than made?

A Contingency Model explanation

The Contingency Model provides a meaningful framework for understanding these seemingly incomprehensible results, and it enables

TABLE 8–1.   Correlations Between Years of Experience and Group Performance. Source: Fiedler, 1970. Reprinted by permission of Academic Press.

	Correlation Coefficient	N
Belgian Navy Study	.10[a]	24
(.08, .13, −.05, .12)		
Military Academy Study	−.21[a]	16
(.03, −.32, −.30, −.21, .42)		
Assistant Postmasters	−.53[a]	19
Superintendents of Mail	−.13	20
Asst. Supts. of Mail	−.12	19
Second-Level Supervisors	.24	23
First-Level Supervisors	−.13	180
Research Chemists	.12	18
Craft Shop Foremen	−.28	11
Meat Department Managers	.09	21
Grocery Department Managers	.33	24
Production Department Foremen	−.18	10
Median Correlation	−.12	385

[a] Only median correlations are listed for these studies.

us to develop a more effective method for utilizing leadership experience and training programs in the future. We will expand on this important theme in the remainder of this chapter.

Note first of all that leadership training has been based on the common assumption that the leader should have as much influence and control as possible. The more influence and control he enjoys, the better, presumably, he will be able to motivate his group members, and the better he will be able to guide and direct them in performing their specific tasks. For this reason, many human relations courses explicitly aim to make the leader more sensitive to the needs of others and to his own impact on them so that he can motivate and direct them more effectively. These courses also provide models and guidelines for handling disciplinary cases, for resolving conflicts with employees, and for handling a wide variety of interpersonal problems which are likely to arise in the course of the work. Training which emphasizes skills in administrative procedures and technical expertise, thus making the leader less dependent on his subordinates, likewise provides guidelines on how to handle the technical difficulties which may arise on the job. The leader is shown how to troubleshoot, he is told whom to contact if he runs into difficulties, and he is taught how to keep records, order supplies, and prepare work-flow charts. The case studies, the role playing sessions, the discussions, and the lectures reduce the leader's need to devise new solutions to problems; they therefore make the job in effect more structured and the situation correspondingly more favorable.

While most leadership training programs assume that the leader will perform better with more influence and control, the Contingency Model shows that task-motivated people perform best if they have either a great deal of or very little control and influence; relationship-motivated people perform better if their control and influence are moderately high. This extremely important point leads to the curious prediction that leadership training and experience, by increasing the leader's control and influence and hence the favorableness of his situation, may in fact decrease his performance under certain conditions.

To illustrate this point let us again take data from our consumer cooperatives study (Godfrey et al., 1959). These managers were divided into those with high and those with low LPC scores, and then were further divided into those who had relatively little experience with the organization and those who had been in the organization for a relatively long time. The leadership situation had been rated as very favorable on the assumption that the leaders had the appropriate experience and training. We expect better performance from task-motivated (low LPC) leaders in very favorable situations and from relationship-motivated (high LPC) leaders in moderately favorable situations. Experience makes the situation favorable because the leader perceives his task as structured. Lack of experience reduces the task structure and probably also the position power, and thus makes the situation only moderately favorable.

Since the high LPC leaders performed better with less experience than they did with more experience, we must assume that the increase in experience actually decreased the performance of these high LPC managers; since low LPC leaders performed better with relatively much than with relatively little experience, we must assume that experience increased their performance. In other words, the intervening time and experience improved the favorableness of the leadership situation, and it therefore called for a different type of leadership (see Figure 8–2). This has now been substantiated in a study by

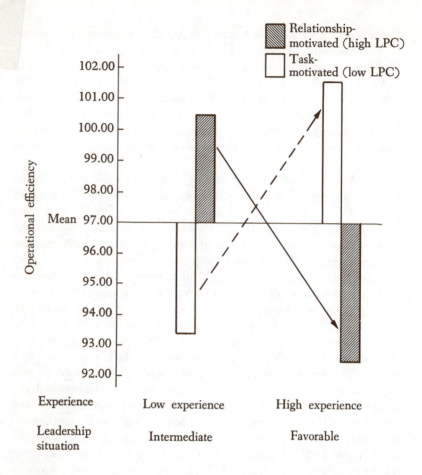

FIGURE 8–2.   Mean Performance Scores (Percent Operating Effi-
ciency/Sales Volume) of Relationship- and Task-Motivated General Managers with Relatively High and Low Levels of Experience in the Cooperative
Federation. Source: Fiedler, 1972b. Reprinted by permission of *Administrative Science Quarterly.*

Bons and Hastings (1973) in which the performance of 19 military
leaders was rated at the time their units were activated and again five
months later.

The effect which leadership experience and training have on
performance will depend upon the type of situation within which the
leader has to operate. The specific predictions of the Contingency

Model for the effects of training (or experience) are shown in Figure 8–3.

Empirical evidence on the effect of training

The first study which suggested that the favorableness of the leadership situation may be affected by the leader's experience was conducted by McNamara (1968). His investigation involved principals of elementary and secondary schools in the province of Alberta, Canada.

McNamara divided the principals in his study into those with less than two years of experience and into those with three or more years of experience. He further divided them into those with high and with low LPC scores. The effectiveness of the elementary schools was rated by school superintendents and their staffs; that of secondary schools was based on the average achievement test score of ninth- and twelfth-grade students in the various schools on a provincewide test. McNamara then computed the average performance scores of experienced and inexperienced principals with high and with low LPC scores. His findings are shown in Figure 8–4.

FIGURE 8–3.   Summary of Hypotheses Regarding the Effects of Training and Experience. Source: Fiedler, 1973. Copyright 1973 by the American Psychological Association and reproduced by permission.

Favorableness of situation for experienced leader	Performance level of leaders with adequate experience		Favorableness of situation for inadequately experienced leader	Performance level of leaders without adequate experience		Predicted effect of training and experience for previously untrained leader
	LPC			LPC		LPC
	High	Low		High	Low	
Very favorable	Poor	Good	Moderate	Good	Poor	High decreases Low increases
Moderately favorable	Good	Poor	Unfavorable	Poor	Good	High increases Low decreases
Unfavorable	Poor	Good	Very unfavorable	Good?	Poor?	High decreases Low increases

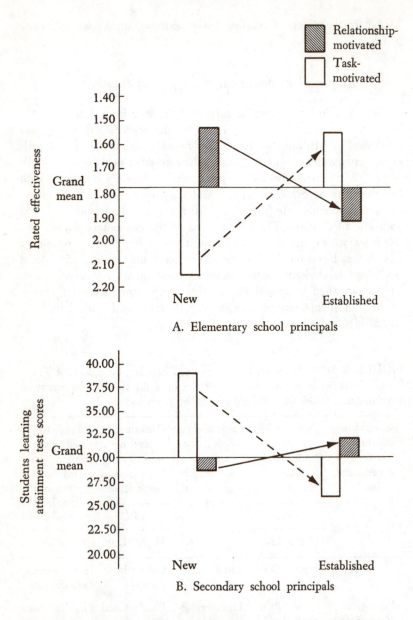

A. Elementary school principals

B. Secondary school principals

FIGURE 8–4.   The Effect of Experience on the Average Performance of Relationship- and Task-Motivated Elementary and Secondary School Principals. Source: Fiedler, 1972b. Reprinted by permission of *Administrative Science Quarterly*.

There is a reversal in performance in both the elementary and the secondary schools. In the sample of elementary school principals, the best performers were the inexperienced principals with high LPC scores and the experienced principals with low LPC scores. The opposite was the case in secondary schools. Here the best performers were inexperienced principals with low LPC scores but experienced principals with high LPC scores. These data are difficult to understand unless we carefully consider the situational favorableness for experienced and inexperienced elementary- and secondary-school principals.

The elementary schools in the McNamara sample are quite small, having an average of 13 teachers. The principal has relatively high position power; he supervises few staff members, and considering the facts that he is dealing with elementary-school pupils and that the curriculum and policy decisions tend to be made at the school super-intendent's level, it seems likely that the situation is highly favorable for the experienced principal. He knows his staff and he knows how the system operates (probably octant i). In these very favorable situations we would expect the low LPC leaders to perform better than the high LPC leaders, and this is indeed the case here (see the left side of Figure 8–4a).

The inexperienced principal undoubtedly faces a less favorable situation. He does not yet know the ropes, and he must still improvise every time a new situation arises. His relationship with and his power over his staff members may also still be fairly tenuous. Hence, his situation is only moderately favorable (probably octant iv). This means that the high LPC leaders should perform better than the low LPC leaders, which is again the case. This implies, of course, that the experience obtained by high LPC principals actually decreases their performance, while experience increases the performance of low LPC principals.

The secondary schools are organizations with two levels of administration, namely that of the school principal and that of the departments within the school. The schools are fairly large, having up to 40 teachers, and the principal also has to deal with teenagers who are notoriously difficult to handle. Moreover, the secondary school principal generally has to interact with various civic, governmental, and parent organizations, and he must make policy on a variety of questions which arise. Thus, although he has moderately high position power, his task is likely to be unstructured, and the relations with those with whom he works are likely to be more tenuous. The experienced secondary school principal's leadership situation is therefore likely to be only moderately favorable (perhaps octant IV). The situation will be unfavorable for the inexperienced principal who must deal with a whole host of problems for the first time (octant VIII) and therefore cannot realistically assert his position power.

According to the Contingency Model, we would expect the high LPC leader to perform better in moderately favorable situations, where he has experience in his job, and the low LPC leader to perform better in unfavorable situations (Figure 8–4b). In the case of secondary schools, experience benefits the high LPC leader, but it is detrimental to the performance of the low LPC leader.

The interpretation of the McNamara data is admittedly quite speculative, although it is very difficult to account for these complex findings in any other meaningful fashion. These data did give rise to hypotheses which have now been tested on a variety of groups (Fiedler, 1972a).

New studies

Before going further, let us for a moment consider the effect of training on situational favorableness. It seems highly likely that a person who is technically untrained, or whose experience and training are insufficient, will experience the task as unstructured. (The skeptical reader without baking experience might try the highly structured task of making crepes suzettes by just following a cookbook. This exercise will make it quite clear that any task, no matter how structured, can present considerable difficulties to the untutored.) In effect, training and experience structure the task in the sense that various actions become routine and that the individual no longer has to improvise or originate methods for performing the task. We might predict, therefore, that task-relevant training and experience will make the situation more favorable in the task-structure dimension. This hypothesis was tested in four recent studies.

The first study (Csoka and Fiedler, 1972; Fiedler, 1972a) was conducted in cooperation with an army field artillery group and involved 55 section chiefs and their gun crews. The second dealt with 58 naval aviation maintenance shops, the third with 60 army training companies, and the fourth with 52 mess halls. In each case, performance was evaluated by two or more of each leader's superiors. All tasks were rated as structured, and all leaders considered to have high position power.

In addition to their LPC and Group Atmosphere scores, leaders also were asked to indicate the number of weeks of leadership training they had received—both along human relations lines and in the form of technical training. The leaders were also asked to indicate the amount of time they had spent in various leadership positions. Almost all of the leaders' training was concerned with the technical aspects of handling and maintaining the equipment. It was primarily designed to improve the leader's technical expertise rather than his ability to manage his subordinates. Only the company commanders reported having received extensive human relations training.

Each of the four sets of groups was divided into those with relatively good and those with poor leader-member relations, as indicated by the Group Atmosphere score. Groups in which the leader had received relatively much training were considered to be situations with high task structure while groups in which the leader had received little training were defined as equivalent to having, *for that leader,* low task structure.

Most military units have leaders whose formal position power is high. However, a situation in which the leader neither knows the task well nor has good relations with his men presents additional difficulties. The leader cannot depend upon his men to help him and he does not have enough expertise to direct them in how to do the job. He therefore really has (and sees himself as having) little position power. You cannot very well control and discipline a man for poor work if you cannot tell him how to do his job. Hence, such a situation is likely to be very unfavorable (octant VIII), and low LPC leaders would perform better than high LPC leaders under these conditions. A situation in which the leader-member relations are good and the leader is trained falls into octant I, and a situation with good leader-member relations but an untrained leader would be equivalent to octant III. In both of these conditions, the low LPC leader should excel. In a moderately favorable situation in which the leader-member relations are poor and the leader is adequately trained (octant V) the high LPC leader should be superior.

The results of the four studies were in high agreement and support the predictions of the theory. We again found that the leaders with relatively little training, taken as a group, perform about as well as leaders with relatively much training. Moreover, when leader-member relations are poor, the task-motivated leaders without training tend to perform better than task-motivated leaders with relatively much training; relationship-motivated leaders without training performed less well than relationship-motivated leaders with training.

A laboratory experiment • The effect of training on task-motivated and relationship-motivated leaders can also be shown in laboratory situations. Chemers and his associates (1973) assembled 32 groups of ROTC cadets. Half the leaders of these three-man groups were given training in deciphering and decoding coded messages while the other half were given no training. As it turned out, the groups felt under considerable pressure and the Group Atmosphere scores were substantially below those normally obtained in laboratory studies. Since the leaders were given relatively little power, the untrained leaders were operating in octant VIII, the least favorable conditions in which task-motivated leaders generally perform best. The trained leaders operated in octant VI in which relationship-motivated leaders are expected to perform better. The effects on group performance were in the expected direction and highly significant. There can be little doubt, therefore, that training has different effects on relationship- and task-motivated leaders and that the Contingency Model provides a reasonable explanation for these complex findings.

The effect of previous leadership experience on group performance • Csoka (1972a,b) also analyzed whether the effect of leadership experience would be similar to the effects of training. He used the same four sets of military units on which he had done his study of leadership training and found similar results, but with one important difference: People who are not very bright apparently do not learn from their experience. It is always nice to find old adages supported by empirical data!

Csoka's findings showed that only the relatively intelligent leaders in each of these groups profited from their experience, that is, for these individuals the effects of training and of experience were virtually identical. The less intelligent leaders, no matter how much experience they may have had, performed in the same way as those who had received very little training. In other words, the relatively dull leader's control and influence, and hence his situational favorableness, did not improve with experience.

For leaders whose relations with members are good the situation is highly favorable only if they are bright as well as experienced. For the leaders whose relations with group members are relatively poor, the situation will be moderately favorable only if they are bright as well as experienced, but it will be unfavorable if they are inexperienced, whether or not they are bright, or if they are experienced and relatively unintelligent. This is a very important point, as we shall see in the next chapter, since it means that a situation does not become more favorable with increasing experience unless the leader is intelligent enough to profit from his experience.

SUMMARY

This chapter has considered some of the theoretical issues in the interpretation of leadership training, experience, and rotation. Basing our argument on the Contingency Model, which says that the leader's motivational orientation and his situation interact to determine his effectiveness, we have reconceptualized the psychological meaning of training and leadership experience as a way of giving the leader a more favorable leadership situation, one which gives him more control and influence. The effects of an increase in favorableness on performance will be mediated by the motivational orientation of the leader.

This interpretation is supported by a wide variety of studies that show why previous studies of leadership training and experience have failed to find across-the-board improvement. We have also shown that the specific points of the Contingency Model provide quite accurate guidelines for predicting whether leadership training and experience will be beneficial or detrimental to the performance of the organization.

REFERENCES

Blake, R. R., and J. S. Mouton. *The Managerial Grid*. Gulf, 1964.

Bons, P. M., and L. L. Hastings. "Leader misperception of leader-member relations and task performance as a function of LPC." Paper presented at the Western Psychological Association Meetings, April 11–14, 1973.

Bunker, D. "Individual applications of laboratory training." *Journal of Applied Science* 3 (1967): 505–24.

Campbell, J. P., M. D. Dunnette, E. E. Lawler, III, and K. E. Weick. *Managerial Behavior, Performance, and Effectiveness*. McGraw-Hill, 1970.

Chemers, M. M., R. W. Rice, E. Sundstrom, and W. M. Butler. "Leader LPC, training, and effectiveness: An experimental examination." Paper presented to the Southern Illinois University Leadership Symposium, May 17–18, 1973.

Csoka, L. S. "A validation of the Contingency Model approach to leadership experience and training." Technical Report No. 72–32. Organizational Research Group, University of Washington, 1972a.

Csoka, L. S. "Intelligence: A critical variable for leadership experience." Technical Report No. 72–34. Organizational Research Group, University of Washington, 1972b.

Csoka, L. S., and F. E. Fiedler. "The effect of military leadership training: A test of the Contingency Model." *Organizational Behavior and Human Performance* 8 (1972): 395–407.

Dunnette, M., and J. Campbell. "Laboratory education: Impact on people and organizations." *Industrial Relations* 8 (1968): 127.

England, G. W. "Personal value systems of American managers." *Academy of Management Journal* 10 (1967): 53–68.

Fiedler, F. E. "The effect of leadership and cultural heterogeneity on group performance: A test of the Contingency Model." *Journal of Experimental Social Psychology* 2 (1966): 237–64.

Fiedler, F. E. "Leadership experience and leader performance: Another hypothesis shot to hell." *Organizational Behavior and Human Performance* 5 (1970): 1–14.

Fiedler, F. E. "Kann man 'führen' wirklich lernen?" *Rationeller Handel* (May 1971).

Fiedler, F. E. "Predicting the effects of leadership training and experience from the Contingency Model." *Journal of Applied Psychology* 56 (1972a): 114–19.

Fiedler, F. E. "The effects of leadership training and experience: A Contingency Model interpretation." *Administrative Science Quarterly* 17 (1972b): 453–75.

Fiedler, F. E. "Predicting the effects of leadership training and experience from the Contingency Model: A clarification." *Journal of Applied Psychology* 57 (1973): 110–13.

Fiedler, F. E., and M. M. Chemers. "Group performance under experienced and inexperienced leaders: A validation experiment." Group Effectiveness Research Laboratory, University of Illinois, Urbana, 1968.

Fiedler, F. E., S. M. Nealey, and M. T. Wood. "The effects of training on performance of post office supervisors." Unpublished manuscript, University of Illinois, Urbana, 1968.

Fleishman, E. A., E. F. Harris, and H. E. Burtt. *Leadership and Supervision in Industry.* Educational Research Monograph No. 33. Personnel Research Board, Ohio State University, 1955.

Godfrey, E. P., F. E. Fiedler, and D. M. Hall. *Boards, Managers, and Company Success.* Interstate Press, 1959.

House, R. J. "T-group education and leadership effectiveness: A review of the empirical literature and a critical evaluation." *Personnel Psychology* 20 (1967): 1–32.

McNamara, V. D. "Leadership, staff, and school effectiveness." Unpublished doctoral dissertation, University of Alberta, 1968.

Odiorne, G. S. "The need for an economic approach to training." *Journal of the American Society of Training Directors* 18 (1964): 3–12.

Schein, E. H. *Organizational Psychology.* Prentice-Hall, 1965.

Increasing
Leadership
Effectiveness
9

This concluding chapter provides some general guidelines for applying the Contingency Model to the improvement of organizational leadership. We have shown that the effectiveness of a group or organization depends upon the proper match between the leader's personality and the degree to which the situation provides him with control and influence, the "favorableness of the situation." Task-motivated leaders tend to perform best in very favorable and unfavorable situations while relationship-motivated leaders perform best in moderately favorable situations.

In its simplest terms, effective organizational leadership therefore boils down to assigning and keeping task-motivated (low LPC) leaders in very favorable and unfavorable situations, and relationship-motivated (high LPC) leaders in moderately favorable situations. In practice, however, difficulties arise because we have to deal with a dynamic system in which situational favorableness constantly changes. The leader's control and influence increase as he gains in experience, as he obtains training, as he improves his relations with subordinates, and as he increases his stature with his superiors. His control and influence decrease as he takes on new and unfamiliar assignments, as he gets subordinates who differ from him in ethnic or racial background, and as he is given tasks for which his intellectual resources are inadequate.

Typically, leadership training has attempted to change the leader's behavior toward his subordinates. Why, then, could we not change the motivational pattern, reflected by the LPC score, so that

140

the leader's personality will fit the job? This is the approach most leadership training programs have followed. As we have said before, it is undoubtedly possible to modify personality and motivational structure, but the cost of such efforts is considerable and the probability of success is low. Such a training program would be tantamount to psychotherapy. Getting an individual to change his personality so that it will match the demands of a particular supervisory position simply does not seem appropriate or practical at this time. For this reason we shall devote the remainder of this chapter to alternative methods of improving organizational leadership. The reader should be clearly aware of the fact that some of these recommendations are quite speculative, while others are based on sound empirical evidence. They are presented not as a recipe, but as possible new approaches to old problems.

ORGANIZATIONAL OPTIONS

Experience

The simplest option the organization has is to let time take its course. The basic problem we must keep in mind in developing a comprehensive system of leadership utilization, therefore, is the effect of time on situational favorableness. Generally speaking, time and the concomitant experience increase the leader's control and influence. The situation which is only moderately favorable for the inexperienced leader is highly favorable for the experienced leader. The situation which is moderately favorable for the experienced leader is unfavorable for the inexperienced leader (see Figure 8–3).[1]

Let us take as an illustration the situation which is *very favorable for the experienced leader* and therefore only moderately favorable for the inexperienced leader. As we can see in Figure 9–1, the task-

1. *In developing a comprehensive leadership utilization program, we will of course need basic data for each person and each situation. These data, to recapitulate, are:*

   1) *The leader's (or prospective leader's) LPC score, some measure of his intelligence or ability to handle the job, his previous experience and training, and, insofar as this can be established, his history of getting along with his subordinates.*

   2) *The leadership position's task structure, position power, and the composition of the group in terms of its racial, ethnic, and technical heterogeneity. We may also wish to have the group members' intelligence and ability scores, as well as the history of the group's relations with its management.*

motivated leader performs very poorly at first, but his performance improves with experience. The relationship-motivated leader performs best at first, when he lacks experience, but over time his performance decreases to the level of the inexperienced low LPC leader. This is schematically shown in Figure 9–1a and represents essentially what we can expect in the absence of training or any other organizational intervention. Figure 9–1b shows the effect of experience in a situation which would "normally" be moderate, that is, of moderate favorableness for the trained and experienced leader. Note here that the curves for high and for low LPC leaders are simply reversed.

Let us now consider a number of options which involve active intervention for the purpose of improving organizational performance.

Rotation

In many organizations, particularly in large companies and the military services, job rotation for management personnel is a common method for providing a wide range of experience to the manager and for cross-fertilization of ideas throughout the company.

As we have seen, time on the job affects the favorableness of the situation. The more experience a bright leader has, the more likely he is to have learned how to deal with the various aspects of the job. The longer he is on the job, the fewer will be the crises which he has not already encountered. In other words, experience on the job increases situational favorableness.

This, as seen in the last chapter, means that the leaders who are outstanding when they are inexperienced, gradually will tend to become mediocre or poor as they settle into a routine which no longer presents challenges. There are other leaders, however, who increase in effectiveness over time as they become more skilled and more acquainted with the routine and not-so-routine problems which the job presents. It is obvious that these latter managers should be left on the job longer since they become increasingly more effective, while the first type should be rotated to new, more challenging jobs at the appropriate time (see Figure 9–2).

The question is, of course, what the "appropriate" time for rotations is and should we condemn the other managers (who become better with time) to life on the same job with no chance of promotion?

The appropriate time on the job will obviously vary with the complexity of the task, the intelligence and ability of the leader, and

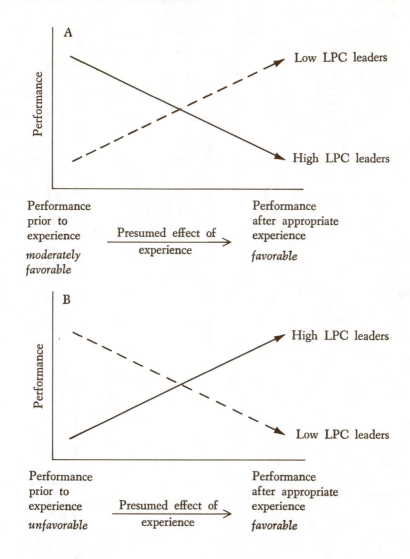

FIGURE 9–1.   Expected Performance of High and Low LPC Leaders Before and After Experience in Normally Favorable Situations.

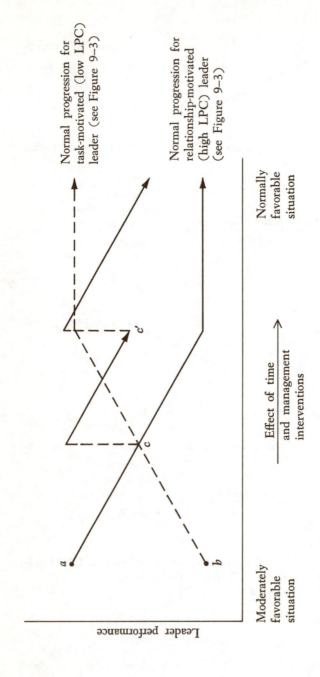

FIGURE 9–2.   Expected Effects of Timely Rotation Policy on the Performance of High and Low LPC Leaders. Point *a* on This Graph Indicates the Initial Level of Performance by Relationship-Motivated (High LPC) Leaders, Point *b* Indicates Initial Performance by Task-Motivated Leaders. Points *c* and *c'* Show the Optimal Point in Time for Rotating High LPC Leaders. Low LPC Leaders Should be Rotated Less Often.

the characteristics of his group members. In the future, we may well be able to say how many months or years of experience various types of leaders ought to have before rotation. Until then we must recommend that each organization determine the proper amount of experience for its own managers. The steps are quite simple.

1) Determine the LPC scores of managers.
2) Carefully measure their performance.
3) Plot the average performance of high and of low LPC managers over time to determine roughly when their performance curves cross (point c in Figure 9–2).
4) In a normally favorable situation, rotate high LPC leaders to similar jobs within the organization and permit low LPC leaders to remain on the job for a longer period of time. In a normally moderate situation, rotate the low LPC leaders at a faster rate than high LPC leaders.

Most leaders obviously should be reassigned or promoted when they have reached the point where their performance declines below the average of the group. The other types of leaders should not be deprived of promotion, however.

They can be helped to become more competent in a shorter period of time by a number of measures. Their job can be made less complex, they can be promoted to higher positions which are similar in situational favorableness, or they can be given intensive training.

Training

Leadership training essentially is leadership experience compressed in time. We distill the experiences of others into rules and guidelines, and we simulate typical problems in leadership situations. We role-play them, or we discuss instances or cases in which problems or conflicts have occurred, so that the leader in training will vicariously experience some of these problems prior to meeting them in real life. In effect, training shortens the time otherwise required for leadership experience.

Training will then enable the task-motivated leader in our illustrative case of the "normally" favorable situation to reach his maximum performance more rapidly. By the same token, however, the relationship-motivated leader's performance in this condition will more rapidly *decrease* with training. Obviously, while we should intensively train the task-motivated leader; training the relationship-motivated leader would be highly dysfunctional. The expected effects of training on the performance of these two types of leaders are shown in Figure 9–3.

Figure 9–3a shows the anticipated results of intensively training a task-motivated leader for a "normally" favorable situation. Curve *a* indicates his improvement without training; curve *a'* indicates the expected effect of training on his performance. Figure 9–3b shows the effect of training on the performance of the relationship-motivated (high LPC) leader in the "normally" favorable situation. Here, of course, training will accelerate the time it takes the relationship-motivated leader to become relatively ineffective. (Again, in moderately favorable situations, the treatment of high and low LPC leaders should be reversed.)

As our analyses have shown, people can be overtrained as well as insufficiently trained. While we frequently do not consider the blessings of ignorance, it is not too difficult to see why the untrained leader might, under a given set of conditions, perform better than the leader who has received a great deal of training. Above all, the untrained leader who is forced to rely on his group members for advice has to adopt a conciliatory stance. He must be concerned with retaining the good will of the group in order to assure himself of their assistance and support. A highly trained leader may lose interest or become arrogant and tempt his subordinates to show him that he doesn't really know as much as he thinks he does.

Since leadership training and experience are mixed blessings, it surely behooves the organization to determine, first of all, how much benefit can be derived from an expensive training program. If some leaders perform better without training, why spend the money on training them? If some leaders, after training, perform less well than they did before, they should be shifted to new jobs which provide the challenge the old job had come to lack.

What, then, is the "best" type of leadership training? For those who would benefit from training, we need to ask what kind of training will increase the leader's situational favorableness as quickly as possible by the right amount.

At this point we cannot say with assurance whether a human relations or a technical approach to training will be more effective. It may well be that all approaches are equally effective as long as they increase the individual's control and influence, but this remains to be

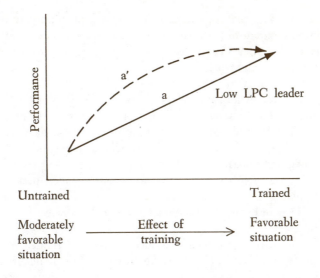

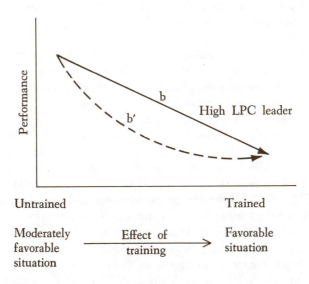

FIGURE 9–3.   The Effect of Training on Task- and Relationship-Motivated Leaders in Situations Which Are "Normally" Favorable.

seen. It seems likely that we can also develop a general-purpose leadership training program to teach the leader how to modify his leadership
situations so that they match his personality. Such a program might
involve the following steps:

1) Obtain measures of task- and relationship-motivation by
means of LPC scores, and then, in the light of the Contingency
Model, carefully discuss the meanings of these measures and
the types of situations in which relationship- and task-motivated leaders tend to perform best.

2) Develop a series of graded exercises which permit each
trainee to experience a very favorable, a moderately favorable,
and an unfavorable situation both as a leader and as a member.

3) Provide guidance and practice for the trainee in diag-
nosing the favorableness of the situation and in modifying it
so that it matches his particular motivational pattern. Provide
feedback on how well the trainee has managed to change the
situational favorableness and complete his job.

We cannot emphasize too strongly that most leaders have a
great deal of influence over their own leadership situation. A leader
may be able to increase his position power by keeping aloof from his
group, by withholding certain types of information, and by insisting
on the prerogatives of his rank; he can also decrease his position power
by being approachable, friendly, and open to subordinates' suggestions,
and by accepting them as his equals. Let us forgo the tempting value
judgment that the latter way of leading groups is always better because it is more democratic and more pleasant. We are talking about
methods for improving leadership performance and not about how to
become a popular leader. Moreover, the distant leader does not always
have less satisfied employees, higher turnover, and a less stable group.
There are, in fact, many people who prefer this type of leadership.
Another method for changing the leadership situation lies in
the way in which the leader himself deals with the task. He can
volunteer for jobs which are highly structured or highly unstructured.
He can structure the tasks himself by carefully planning them in step-
by-step fashion, or, especially if he is relationship-motivated, he can
present the problem to his group members with the invitation that
they help him plan and organize the job.
Which of these types of situations works best is something

which each leader must carefully determine for himself. The organization can assist by providing the leader with accurate feedback on how well he performs under various conditions.

Selection and placement

At first blush, the selection and placement problem seems quite straightforward. Given a group of candidates who are otherwise equally qualified to assume leadership positions in the organization, we could simply select low LPC persons for situations which have been classified as very favorable or as unfavorable, and high LPC persons for situations which are moderately favorable.

On the other hand, though, we must realize that we are selecting these individuals on the assumption that the organization will patiently wait for months or years for them to reach their full potential. In other words, this selection of task-motivated leaders for favorable situations, and relationship-motivated leaders for moderately favorable situations, is a long-run strategy.

If there is an immediate need for effective leadership, a different selection strategy must be considered. We really don't care how well the leaders will perform in the distant future if we need outstanding performance right now. Hence, we will be better served by selecting the relationship-motivated leaders for the "normally" favorable situation (left side of Figure 9–1a) and the task-motivated leaders for the situation which is "normally" moderately favorable. Whether we choose the long-run or the short-run strategy will depend on (A) the urgency of obtaining the best leadership in the shortest possible period of time and (B) how long it will take the task-motivated leader to reach his optimal performance level in the favorable situation and the relationship-motivated leader to reach his optimum in the moderately favorable situation. In unfavorable situations, we will, of course, always want to choose the task-motivated leader if we primarily seek optimum performance, even though his interpersonal relations in highly unfavorable situations tend to be poor.

Ethnically and racially mixed groups

It is well known that individuals in culturally and ethnically mixed groups are more likely to have conflict and misunderstandings than individuals who come from a very similar background. It is unfortunate, though not surprising, that heterogeneous groups are therefore more difficult to control. On the whole, however, these groups are about as effective as highly homogeneous groups.

While ethnically and racially mixed groups are clearly less comfortable and more anxiety-arousing for the leader, they also present an opportunity for rational assignment and management policies. If the group presents a less favorable situation, the time required for the leader to establish his control and influence will be longer than for a highly homogeneous group. The relationship-motivated leader will therefore remain effective for a longer period of time in normally favorable situations (in which the trained and experienced leader's situation is favorable). The task-motivated leader will remain effective longer in normally moderately favorable situations.

The effect of assigning a leader to a highly heterogeneous group is shown in Figure 9–4. A recent analysis of data from culturally mixed groups by Bons and Hastings (1973) supports this prediction.

Organizational engineering

Finally, the organization may opt for a modification in certain aspects of a leadership job in order to increase an individual's performance. This is frequently done because many managers cannot be transferred to other jobs for some reason. Their technical knowledge may make them indispensable, they may have a great deal of seniority, or they may have friends in high places. Under these conditions the organization may try to fit the job to the individual.

To obtain the best results with such a procedure, we need to consider carefully which specific aspects of the managerial job will strengthen and which will weaken the leader's control and influence. The particular methods for modifying the favorableness of the situation will differ from organization to organization, but a few examples will illustrate what can be done.

1) We may, for example, be able to assign the individual subordinates who are his juniors in age and experience. This will increase his control and influence. Assigning to him old, experienced hands who are nearly his equals or his seniors in job knowledge and age will decrease his control over the group. We may assign him individuals who are similar or who

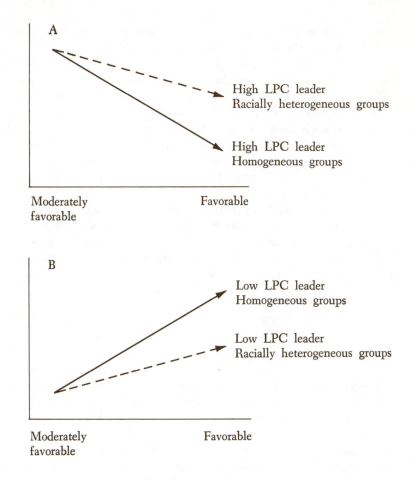

FIGURE 9–4.   The Effect of Group Composition on the Performance of Relationship- and Task-Motivated Leaders.

differ in technical background, age, sex, and race; we may give him compliant subordinates or habitual troublemakers. Also, we may give him an assistant who has the skills he himself lacks.

2) We can give some managers very specific step-by-step instructions on how the job is to be accomplished; we can provide them with standard operating instructions and guidelines and specific target goals to be met. We can give others

jobs which are unstructured, or jobs where the execution is left to the individual and his subordinates.

3) We can increase the position power of the leader by increasing his rank, by giving him authority to mete out rewards and penalties, by supporting all of his decisions, by channeling all information through him. We can decrease his position power by curtailing his power to reward and punish, by intimating that the organization's support is tentative, by requiring him to consult with his group members on various issues, or by sharing information with group members as well as with the leader.

It should be obvious that all of these proposed changes in the job may be neither feasible nor appropriate on all occasions, but these examples should be considered by any organization attempting to provide a leadership situation which permits the individual to perform at his best.

CONCLUSION

The central idea we have tried to convey in this chapter and throughout this book is that the Contingency Model opens up a host of new options for dealing with leadership problems and for improving leadership performance. None of these options can be applied uncritically and blindly, and not all of them will be appropriate in any one situation. Some may even be impossible or undesirable under certain conditions. But almost every leadership situation we can imagine permits the exercise of at least one or two of these alternative strategies to modify the favorableness of the leadership situation, and hence the performance of the leader. We hope that this book may enable the reader to work out ways to make his own organization more effective.

REFERENCES

Bons, P. M., and L. L. Hastings. "Leader misperception of leader-member relations and task performance as a function of LPC." Paper presented at the Western Psychological Association Meetings, April 11–14, 1973.

Appendix

10

RATING FORM TO DETERMINE
JOB TASK STRUCTURE
UTILIZED BY J. G. HUNT [1]

I. Please rate according to the instructions in the follow-ing sections those jobs which you and the researcher have agreed are a representative cross section of jobs in your company.

II. You will note that there are four dimensions on which each job is to be rated. Each dimension is described on a separate sheet. Please rate all jobs on a given dimension before going to the next dimension. In other words, jobs are to be rated on each dimension independently of the way they are rated on other di-mensions.

III. (A) In order to help you in your rating, you will note that there is a graphic scale (ranging from 1 to 11) for each dimension with job titles arranged below the horizontal line so as to cover most of the points on the scale. These are called "anchor jobs."

(B) All anchor jobs, with the exception of two, have been evaluated by a panel of judges, and general

1. Source: Fiedler, F. E. A Theory of Leadership Effectiveness. Mc-Graw-Hill, 1967, Appendix D, pp. 282–291. Reprinted by permission of McGraw-Hill and J. G. Hunt.

agreement has been reached that the jobs belong where they are shown on the scale. These jobs were selected from among one hundred because of the high inter-judge agreement.

(C) A short description of each job on the scale is included on the same page. This is the same description that the judges used in rating the jobs.

IV. When rating the selected jobs in your company, please keep the description of the anchor jobs in mind and rate your jobs in relation to these anchor jobs.

V. Note that in many cases there are different anchor jobs as job dimensions change.

VI. (A) In order to simplify your rating work, it is suggested that you list (on the last sheet clipped to these) your company jobs to be rated. (Note that each line on this sheet is lettered and this will be the job letter.) Then it is suggested that you familiarize yourself with the dimension you are going to rate and the anchor-job descriptions.

(B) After doing this, place the letter corresponding to the job you are rating above the anchor job which most nearly corresponds to it for the dimension you are rating.

(C) After you have done this for each job, check to see that you have placed them where you think they belong. This may mean you will rearrange some of your earlier placements. After you are satisfied that you have rated the jobs the way you want them in relation to each other and in relation to the anchor jobs, do the same thing for the next dimension. Please do not refer to job ratings on earlier dimensions when rating on later dimensions, however.

VII. Do not worry if you have not covered every number on the scale. It may be that you are dealing with a narrow range of jobs. Also, you will note that there are parts of some of the scales which have no anchor jobs, because none were found to fall consistently on those parts of the scale. If you believe some of your jobs should lie at these points, it is all right to place them there. Please make sure, however, you have placed your jobs above one of the eleven points on the scale and not in between these points.

DIMENSION I

Goal clarity

This is the degree to which the requirements of a job (the tasks or duties which typically make up the job) are clearly stated or known to people performing the job.

Read the job descriptions for Dimension I. Then think of yourself as the person assigned the job and ask yourself how clear *what* you are to do is to you. Do not include *how* you are to do the job. There is another dimension.

To rank this dimension, assume that the *lower* the scale number, the *lower* the goal clarity (the less clear the goals of the job).

1	I.	Idle millionaire
2	II.	Hobo
3		
4		
5	III.	Train director
	IV.	Private detective
	V.	Receiving stores supervisor
6	VI.	Educational director
7	VII.	Notary public
8	VIII.	Canvas cover repair foreman
9	IX.	Bench carpenter
10	X.	Chili maker
11	XI.	Axle assembler

Place the letters of jobs corresponding in structure to the anchor jobs shown on the scale directly above those anchor jobs. If there is no anchor job above the number on the scale, you can still place your job there if desired.

JOB DESCRIPTIONS FOR DIMENSION I

I. Idle millionaire.

II. Hobo. Note: Since no job evaluated by the judges was found to extend beyond 5 on this dimension, these two "jobs" have been added in an effort to broaden the scale. It may well be that some of your jobs approach these two on this dimension. You may supply your own descriptions for these two jobs.

III. Train director. Directs switching of railroad traffic entering or leaving yards to regulate movements of trains in conformity with traffic schedules and safety regulations. Signals switching directions to towerman by manipulating controls from central control room.

IV. Private detective. Performs private police work to protect property by detecting thievery, shoplifting, or dishonesty among employees or patrons of a business establishment or other private organization.

V. Receiving and stores supervisor. Supervises workers engaged in receiving and storing production materials in an industrial establishment. Note: While the above three are different jobs, they were given the same rating on this dimension.

VI. Educational director. Plans, organizes and administers training programs designed to promote efficiency through instruction of new employees in firm's policies, systems and routines. Instructs foremen in vocational training methods.

VII. Notary public. Administers oaths or affirmations where required, issues summonses for witnesses in cases before courts or other persons authorized to examine witnesses. Takes affidavits on request.

VIII. Canvas cover repair foreman. Supervises a group of workers who repair tents, awnings, and canvas covers used to protect various objects, such as motors and instruments.

IX. Bench carpenter (woodworking). Works at a bench in an industrial firm and fits and assembles prefabricated wooden sections; or cuts, shapes, fits, and assembles wooden sections according to blueprints and sketches, performing general carpentry duties, such as sawing, planing, jointing, fitting, and nailing.

X. Chili maker. Cooks specified amounts of ground meat, chili, spices, chopped onions, garlic, and beef tallow in a steam-jacketed kettle to make chili and ladles from kettle into cans. All ingredients weighed out by chili maker or according to his formula.

XI. Axle assembler (auto manufacturing). Secures front- or

rear-axle subassemblies to chassis springs on final assembly line. Bolts subassembly in place using wrenches
and power-driven nut-tightening tools.

DIMENSION II

Goal-path multiplicity

This is the degree to which the problems encountered in the
job can be solved by a variety of procedures (number of different paths
to the goal—number of alternatives in performing the job—number of
different ways the problems typically encountered in the job can be
solved).

Read the job descriptions for Dimension II. Then think of
yourself as the person assigned the job, and remembering that you have
already evaluated the job in terms of *what* is expected, now shift and
think of *how* you are to do the job. How many ways are there to accomplish the goal? To what extent is planning necessary to decide
how to do the job?

To rank this dimension, assume that the *lower* the scale number, the *lower* the goal-path multiplicity (the less paths there are to
the goal).

1	I.	Date puller
2	II.	Off-line assembler
3	III.	Billing clerk
4	IV.	Form builder
5	V.	Drafting clerk
6	VI.	Receiving and stores supervisor
7	VII.	Dance hall inspector
	VIII.	Chief clerk
8	IX.	Buyer
9	X.	Broadcast director
10	XI.	Research engineer
11		

Place letters of jobs corresponding in structure to anchor jobs
shown on the scale directly above anchor jobs. If there are no anchor
jobs above the number on the scale, you can still place your job there
if desired.

JOB DESCRIPTIONS FOR DIMENSION II

I.   Date puller. Cuts open dates, removes the stones, and cuts the dates into pieces for use in making candy.

II. Off-line assembler (auto manufacturing). Assembles units, such as windshields and lights, which are later placed on the automobile chassis as it passes over the assembly lines. Uses screwdriver, power-driven nut tightener, and other hand tools.

III. Billing clerk. Prepares statements, bills, and invoices, by hand or on a typewriter, to be sent to customers, showing an itemized account of the amount they owe. Obtains information from purchase orders, sales and charge slips or other records. Addresses envelopes and inserts bills preparatory to mailing. Checks billings with accounts receivable ledger.

IV. Form builder (aircraft and auto manufacturing). Builds forms, fixtures, jigs, or templates of wood or metal for use as guides or standards by other workers in mass production of cars or planes. Studies blueprint of part for which fixture is to be built and lays out, cuts, and assembles component pieces of wood or metal. Checks and measures finished assembly against blueprint.

V.   Drafting clerk. Draws and letters organization charts, schedules, and graphs. Uses simple drafting instruments such as ruling pen, lettering pen, and straightedge to produce neat, legible charts and graphs.

VI. Receiving and stores supervisor. See job description for Dimension I.

VII. Dance hall inspector. A member of the police force who inspects all dance halls for licenses and for conduct of patrons. Enforces regulations concerning such places and reports on the manner in which each is operated.

VIII. Chief clerk. Coordinates the clerical work of an establishment, directing performance of such services as the keeping of personnel and time records, standardizing operating procedures for clerical work, and purchasing and keeping inventories of clerical supplies and equipment. Directs work of several subordinate office managers. Note: While the above two jobs are different, they were given the same rating on this dimension.

IX. Buyer (retail or wholesale trade). Purchases merchandise within budgetary limitations in sufficient quantity and with sufficient appeal to sell rapidly. Assigns selling price to merchandise and initiates procedures such as price reductions to promote the sale of surplus or slow-moving items.

X. Broadcast director. Supervises broadcasting of specific radio programs. Formulates general policies to be followed in preparing and broadcasting programs. Keeps expenditures for producing programs within budgetary limits and creates and develops program ideas.

XI. Research engineer. Conducts engineering research concerned with processing a particular kind of commodity with a view to improving present products and discovering new products or to improving and discovering new machinery for production purposes. Examines literature on subject. Plans and executes experimental work to check theories advanced. Consults with other engineers to get their ideas. Prepares report of findings.

DIMENSION III

Decision verifiability

This is the degree to which the "correctness" of the solutions or decisions typically encountered in a job can generally be demonstrated by appeal to authority or authoritative source (e.g., the census of 1960), by logical procedures (e.g., mathematical demonstration), or by feedback (e.g., examination of consequences of decision, as in action tasks).

Read the job descriptions for Dimension III. Then think of yourself as the person assigned the job and ask yourself to what extent it is possible for you or others evaluating your work to know whether the job has been done "correctly" or not. A time sequence is implied here. For some jobs it is never possible to know the correctness of the decision. For other jobs it is possible to know but only after a long period of time, say, one year or more. For others it is possible to know immediately or within a one-year period.

To rank this dimension, assume that the *lower* the scale number, the *lower* the decision verifiability (the less ways there are to verify job decisions).

1		
2	I.	Social welfare research worker
3		
4	II.	Design engineer
5	III.	Service director
6	IV.	Buyer
7	V.	Cameraman
8	VI.	Account analyst
9	VII.	Cabinet assembler
	VIII.	File clerk
10	IX.	Off-line assembler
11	X.	Nut and bolt sorter

Place letters of jobs corresponding in structure to anchor jobs shown on the scale directly above anchor jobs. If there is no anchor job above the number on the scale, you can still place your job there if desired.

JOB DESCRIPTIONS FOR DIMENSION III

I. Social welfare research worker. Performs research to facilitate investigation and alleviation of social problems. Gathers facts by reference to selected literature and by consultation. Analyzes data, employing statistical computations, and correlates information. Evaluates social projects or disposition of cases in light of findings. Estimates future needs for services and presents facts significant to formulation of future plans.

II. Design engineer. Creates designs for machinery or equipment. Draws up construction details and determines production methods and standards of performance. Investigates practicability of designs in relation to limitations of manufacturing equipment and gives advice on construction, manufacture, materials, and processes. Experiments with existing machinery to improve design.

III. Service director (retail trade). Supervises all operating and nonselling services of a large store, such as delivery, wrapping, storage, stock keeping, receiving, and alterations. Responsible for care of building and upkeep of equipment, such as elevators.

IV. Buyer (retail or wholesale trade). See job description for Dimension II.

V. Cameraman (motion picture). Photographs anybody or anything of which motion pictures may be required with a motion-picture camera. Specializes in shots from unusual angles and dangerous heights or positions.

VI. Account analyst (banking). Determines and prepares charges to be made against commercial accounts for various services performed by the bank. Prepares reports on status and value of individual accounts for bank officials.

VII. Cabinet assembler (furniture). Assembles by hand the parts of the radio cabinet that have been cut and dressed in the machine department, fastening the joints together with glue or braces at the points of union, and holding them together with clamps.

VIII. File clerk. Keeps correspondence, cards, invoices, receipts, and other records arranged systematically according to subject matter in file cabinets or drawers. Reads information on incoming material and sorts and places it in proper position in filing cabinet. Locates and removes material from cabinet when requested. Note: The above two jobs are different, but they were given the same rating on this dimension.

IX. Off-line assembler (auto manufacturing). See job description for Dimension II.

X. Nut and bolt sorter. Sorts nuts and bolts by hand according to size, length, and diameter. Discards defective pieces.

DIMENSION IV

Solution specificity

This is the degree to which there is generally more than one "correct solution" involved in tasks which typically make up a job.

Some tasks, e.g., arithmetic problems, have only one solution that is acceptable; others have two or more, e.g., a sorting task where items to be sorted have several dimensions; and still others have an almost infinite number of possible solutions, each of which may be equally as good as others. For example, consider human relations problems or many problems managers must make decisions about.

Read the job descriptions for Dimension IV. Then think of yourself as the person who must decide whether tasks typically falling within a given job have been performed correctly or not. Ask yourself how difficult it would be to decide the relative correctness of the task solution of two people who have been assigned a given task as a part of their job and have come up with quite different answers.

Where there are a number of solutions which might be equally acceptable, you are dealing with a job low in solution specificity.

To rank this dimension, assume that the *lower* the scale number, the *lower* the solution specificity (the *more* correct solutions there are).

1	I.	Social welfare research worker
2	II.	Research engineer
3	III.	Dancer
4	IV.	Broadcast news analyst
5	V.	Service manager
6	VI.	Warehouse manager
7	VII.	Cane cutter
8	VIII.	Electrical assembler
9	IX.	Candy-cutting machine girl
10	X.	Dairy maid
11	XI.	Barrel drainer

Place letters of jobs corresponding in structure to anchor jobs shown on the scale directly above anchor jobs.

JOB DESCRIPTIONS FOR DIMENSION IV

I. Social welfare research worker. See job description for Dimension III.

II. Research engineer. See job description for Dimension II.

III. Dancer. Performs dances alone, with a partner, or in a group.

IV. Broadcast news analyst. Analyzes and interprets news from various sources. Prepares copy and broadcasts material over radio station or network.

V. Service manager. Supervises activities of an institution that renders service to the public, such as a business-service, repair-service or personal-service establishment.

VI. Warehouse manager. Manages one or more commercial or industrial warehouses to maintain stocks of material. Directs through intermediate supervisors checking of incoming and outgoing shipments. Keeps stock records and does other clerical tasks. Directs handling and disposition of materials through foremen and establishes and enforces operations procedures according to work requirements.

VII. Cane cutter. Cuts sugarcane in the fields during harvest season using a broad-bladed knife. Pulls off side leaves of several cane stalks with hook at end of knife and cuts the leaves from stalk with knife blade. Cuts through stalk at base of ripe section and places cut stalks in piles.

VIII. Electrical assembler (refrigeration equipment). Installs electrical equipment in refrigerator display cases working from blueprints. Cuts pockets and bores holes in wooden framing of case with electric or hand tools to install wiring and light receptacles. Attaches wires to fixtures and fixtures to receptacles, using hand tools, and tests circuits of completed case for errors in wiring or hookup.

IX. Candy-cutting machine girl. Takes cut candies from cutting machine by hand and arranges them on metal trays ready for wrappers and packers. Picks out imperfect pieces of candy and drops them into a container. When conveyors are used, arranges pieces on conveyor belt as they come from the cutting knives.

X. Dairy maid. Performs lighter types of work on a dairy farm. Milks cows. Separates cream by hand in pans or by machine with a cream separator. Churns butter with a hand churn.

XI. Barrel drainer. Empties water from barrel that has been inspected or weighed by rolling barrel onto a stand and pulling bung from hole by hand.

SUBJECT INDEX

NAME INDEX